BECOMING AUTISM FRIENDLY

A small town's journey towards autism awareness, acceptance and inclusion.

R. L. ROY

Published by Wreckhouse Press
10 Lillington Avenue, PO Box 773
Channel-Port aux Basques, Newfoundland
A0M 1C0 Canada
info@wreckhousepress.com

ISBN 978-0-9948136-1-9
Becoming Autism Friendly: A small town's journey towards autism awareness, acceptance and inclusion by R. L. Roy.

Available via paperback and e-book at:

www.wreckhousepress.com
www.amazon.ca (.com)

and independent book retailers including:

Butterfly Book Boutique (facebook.com/butterflybookboutique/)

WRECKHOUSE
PRESS

Autism Involves Me (AIM) Mission Statement

We are an informal group with the overall purpose of discussing autism, sharing information and offering emotional support. Our goal is to create a sense of unity and help each other wherever possible, because each of us has our own story about how Autism Involves Me.

This book would not be possible without support from the following people.

With special thanks to AIM Directors:

Joan Chaisson and Candace Matthews

With sincere thanks to:

Valerie Francis
Terrence Harvey
Michael Patey
Joanie Sheppard
Kristopher Bragg (Kris' Kustoms)
Niki Carroll (Instructional Resource Teacher)
Tony Leamon (Speech Language Pathologist)
Cathy Lomond (Hotel Port-aux-Basques)
Kayla MacDonald (Doggie Dooz & Cat Groomz)
Peggy McNeil (Port aux Basques Pizza Delight)
David Palmer (Dr. Charles L. LeGrow Health Centre)
Andrew Parsons (Justice Minister MHA for Burgeo-La Poile)
Wanda Ryan Merrigan (Bruce II Sports Centre)
Valerie Parsons (Butterfly Book Boutique)
Todd Strickland (Town Councillor & Deputy Fire Chief)
Jeannette Tobin (First Choice Convenience)

A MESSAGE FROM AIM

The information in this book explains the successful journey of how the Autism Involves Me (AIM) group and our town, Channel-Port aux Basques, became autism friendly. The pilgrimage began with little ideas based on desires from parents of children on the autism spectrum. As these little ideas became realities, bigger dreams began to form, and before we knew it, we were engaged in whole town partnerships.

I am very proud to be a citizen of this autism friendly town, whose residents are always ready to welcome new autistic families or support whatever project our group is involved in at any time. This book details a journey of hard work, dedication and many rewards!

I sincerely hope that you can use this book as your guide to create your own autism friendly community.

Lastly, I would like to say thank you to R. L. Roy for writing this book. I feel she has captured an overall vision of our goals and successes, and she has made it possible for this story to be shared with others so their lives can be accepted and appreciated in their communities.

Joan Chaisson
Director and Co-founder
Autism Involves Me (AIM)

INTRODUCTION

"Change will not come if we wait for some other person or some other time. We are the ones we've been waiting for. We are the change that we seek."

– Barack Obama

If you were going to pick a place to try overhaul the status quo, Channel-Port aux Basques, Newfoundland might be one of the last places you'd choose.

This typical, cute seaside town has a federal ferry service that provides a link to the mainland, but you can actually enter or leave the province without ever setting foot into the town itself. There are less than 4,000 residents, no traffic lights and nothing to recommend it as a testing ground for societal change.

I'm not even sure that was one of the primary goals when Autism Involves Me was founded but it is what they have accomplished, and when considered as a whole, it is a truly remarkable achievement.

I first met Joan Chaisson when I was less than a week into my new job as the lone community reporter covering the Southwest coast. An unassuming, soft spoken woman with a warm smile walked into the reception room, asked for a moment of my time, and said that the hotel directly across the street was about to become Canada's first truly autism-friendly hotel, a story my predecessor had been working on for the paper. Did I want to cover it instead?

It wasn't really a question.

Without exception, every person I interviewed for this book referenced Joan's strength, determination and dedication. Her unfailing kindness and respectful, quiet demeanor mask a cast iron will, and a great deal of AIM's success in making the town an autism friendly one can be attributed directly to her.

That is not to minimize in any way the rest of the group, the local business community and so many others who have poured their heart and soul into the transformation as well, because by and large those people share the exact same traits. Led by Joan, they have proven themselves as a formidable, capable force.

The best thing about this community model they have built is how truly adaptable it is. Many of the resources that were designed specifically for children with autism have also helped others living in the region or even tourists passing through.

One need not necessarily be a child on the autism spectrum to take advantage of the sensory gym or dine out at an autism friendly restaurant. AIM's programs have evolved to assist people of all age ranges, including adults, and helped those tackling different conditions such as anxiety or Aspergers or even Down's Syndrome. The little volunteer group makes its resources available to anyone who asks or may benefit, regardless of whether or not they have autism.

As the children in this town continue to grow, AIM will grow too, developing new programs, perhaps something similar to the Ready, Willing and Able provincial program that matches job seekers with autism to suitable employers. If there's a way to make life more inclusive or people with autism, I have absolutely no doubt AIM will find it.

It has been my privilege to witness the transition of this community and I am honoured that AIM has trusted me to share their work. It's my sincere hope that the story of our little town will not only serve as a practical community guidebook and resource, but as inspiration to drive further change in matters completely unrelated to autism.

We can do it. We really can.

R. L. Roy

CONTENTS

FOREWORD
The people who care

As the room filled slowly with teachers and support staff clutching coffee cups and notebooks, the Educational Psychologist went through timetables, fire alarm procedures and icebreakers before introducing the first speaker of this in-service training day: my daughter, Nuala, had volunteered to give a short presentation about living with ASD, or Autistic Spectrum Disorder.

"My life can be very tough," she said. "Very often people will say I look happy enough but they have no idea how I feel inside."

It was a sobering talk which underlined the need for greater understanding.

School can be a difficult place at the best of times but vulnerable children often struggle in settings where peers and teachers lack the emotional literacy and factual knowledge required to support them. Even in the kindest of company, jokes are difficult to understand, puns and sayings make no sense at all and body language is fraught with misunderstanding.

Who would ever say 'break a leg' to wish you luck? Why do people say, "Oh, look!" and show you their outstretched arm with their index finger pointing? You look at their hand and wonder how you were supposed to know they meant the cat sitting 20 feet away.

Environmental interference can be overwhelming: the bustle, the noise, flickering lights, the smells from the canteen, the way the lines on the window and the carpet fail to match up.

Children respond in a wide variety of ways. Some become angry, some withdraw, some just want to escape. Some cope by clamping on a tight mask and never revealing the truth about their distress until they reach the safety of home where they explode like a time-delay device.

To know one autistic person, the saying goes, is to know *one* autistic person. Every human is a unique individual. Everybody has struggles and talents they share with others, and some that are all their own. It is the willingness to listen and learn what works that makes the difference.

Many autistic people prefer the term Autistic Spectrum Condition (ASC), explaining that the term disorder makes them feel broken or flawed. Condition is a more neutral and holistic description which allows for positives, too.

A sense of pattern so strong it makes asymmetry almost unbearable can also be a superpower. This is what I say to my daughter: When you were young and you started Highland Dancing, you were the smallest in the class by far, but you never missed a beat, not once. You have near-perfect pitch and your drumming is outstanding. Your eye for irregularity is legendary. If anyone loses a tiny object on a gravel path you will find it. Your ability to focus on a topic which interests you means that you have found out and retained more information on Harry Potter than J. K. Rowling ever knew existed. You are already an accomplished artist and composer, and you can maintain focus for longer than most grown ups I know.

To the kids at school who are on the autism spectrum I say this: You may be fantastic at football, or especially thoughtful and affectionate with younger children. Maybe you know lots about trains or comics. Maybe you are fascinated by light and see in it a beauty that eludes most people. You are honest, with a keen sense of fair play. You might find deep comfort in the sounds of your own voice or you might enjoy the sensation from squashing blu-tac. You may find physical touch unbearable, to the point where a hug or a kiss on the cheek make you want to climb out of your skin, but you may be able to compensate by lying under a weighted blanket or squeezing your body through padded rollers.

We are one of those families who live autism on a daily experience. Beyond the diagnostic jargon lies a world of continuous struggles with things that appear to be no big deal to those for whom they are not.

For an autistic person, though, seemingly ordinary situations can pose insurmountable obstacles, and this is the crux: *it needn't be so.*

A modest amount of education can move mountains. Very minor changes can make all the difference in the world.

A recent trip to Newfoundland, Canada was an inspiration and a revelation. Channel-Port aux Basques is a small seaside town with a population of just over 4,000. It is also Canada's only officially accredited autism-friendly town.

Joan Chaisson welcomed us like family and took us on a tour of the local schools, the leisure centre, the shops, the bistro, a church and one of the hotels. What we saw blew us away.

It's not that they spent a fortune – they did not.

A group of parents together with Joan, a recently retired special education teacher, set up a support group which they named AIM (Autism Involves Me) and they persuaded the town to take this motto to heart. The changes they made were groundbreaking, yet simple. Awareness is the key.

Our residence, Hotel Port aux Basques, was the first autism friendly hotel in Canada and possibly in North America. Their website has a walk through video tour so you can see in advance where you will sleep and eat.

"So what?" you may think.

However, for an autistic child, that alone can make the difference between days of deep anxiety and feeling okay about going. Their sensory room is beautifully appointed and some of the rooms have special safety features in case of violent meltdowns under pressure. A high lock and an absence of loose, fragile objects provide endless reassurance to parents who live with constant worry.

The local hairdresser learned how to win the trust of a young lad with severe anxieties and sensory difficulties – he talks the boy through every procedural detail first and gives him a lollipop for each hand to balance out the sensation.

The emergency services have a box of soothing toys which carries instructions for the first responders on the inside of the lid, reminding them to speak in a slow, even voice using short sentences and repeating answers as often as needed.

The restaurants printed pictures on the menu so that non-verbal children can make choices. The Fire Brigade Christmas Parade involves a stretch without sirens or flashing lights. The supermarket has a weekly quiet shopping hour with the music switched off and the lights turned down low. The local hospital is about to unveil its own soothing chill out space.

Many of these things cost very little yet their benefit is likely to transcend their target group. The wider appeal also applies to the resources in sensory rooms in the schools and the fun gym at the leisure centre. It is a joy to watch children of all ages and abilities play in this bright, airy space.

Physical resources are not cheap, it's true. However, much of the fundraising was accomplished by the AIM group itself, and local businesses gave generously.

Joan's passion and her personal dedication are irresistible. She was described to us as a very special lady by the townsfolk, and I could see immediately that they were right. I am proud to say that we have become friends and I hope, one day, to repay her kind hospitality.

One thing I can do right now is to learn from her. There is no reason at all why the model could not be replicated in most towns across the world: the secret is simply to find enough people who care.

In my own village this will be no problem. We are fortunate to live in a close-knit West Highland village not so unlike Channel-Port aux Basques.

We, too, have a ferry port and a thriving fishing industry. We, too, have excellent schools with staff who are deeply invested in the children's well-being. And we, too, have local businesses who put human kindness above everything else.

Plans are already being made to raise funding for sensory rooms. Meetings will take place to determine which businesses to approach with what suggestions. We will need to look at ways in which we can provide training and accreditation.

But the main thing is the realization that parents of autistic children are not on their own. Just getting by and narrowly avoiding major drama on a daily basis is not as good as it gets.

We can do better if we work together to create a more inclusive environment, and awareness is the first step.

Lisa MacDonald
(Nuala's mother)
Scotland

From left: Finlay MacDonald, Lisa MacDonald, Steve Husband and Nuala MacDonald.
© *Courtesy of Lisa MacDonald*

CHAPTER ONE
A safe space to share

On the Southwest corner of a windswept, rocky island province in the North Atlantic two women sat a kitchen table, oblivious to the fact that they were on the cusp of developing a grassroots movement.

One of the women, a mother with a child on the autism spectrum, was feeling a bit lost, lonely and overwhelmed. Her companion was Joan Chaisson, a retired educator who was working with the family as an Applied Behaviour Analysis (ABA) home therapist.

The mother could not have picked a better confidante with whom to share her frustrations. Although Chaisson did not have any autistic children of her own, what she had was an in-depth understanding of the challenges the mother was facing and an innate passion for helping.

Chaisson had been teaching since 1979, a career she more or less fell into after listening to a pitch from a pair of Grenfell College recruiters who visited the vocational school she was attending. Before then, she'd had no intention of getting a college degree.

After graduating from high school at 17, Chaisson killed time at the vocational school in Channel-Port aux Basques, taking clerical courses for a year while waiting to turn 18, at which time she intended to get her permit to start driving school buses for her father's company.

Once the college recruiters left, Chaisson went home and told her surprised parents that she was going to attend colleges and become either

Michael Ksienski, 9 years old, is a gold medal pianist with the Royal Conservatory of Music.

a teacher or a minister. Years later she would make another compulsive but critical decision to study again, traveling to Harlow, England for two semesters to study teaching.

That decision not only made her an invaluable resource for the small community schools on the Southwest Coast of Newfoundland, it kept her constantly employed in a sometimes volatile and uncertain field.

Not long after retiring in June 2009 Chaisson began working one-on-one with a child on the autism spectrum, something she dearly loved. A visit from her son, who lived in Alberta, prompted her and her husband to relocate to Calgary. Once again she took a private job working with a two year old boy named Michael.

Under her care, and in addition to working with a Speech Language Pathologist, Michael made enormous strides. At age nine he achieved gold medal status in the Royal Conservatory of Music for playing the piano in all of Alberta and Northwest Territories in his age group and against neurotypical peers.

During that time in Calgary it wasn't just Michael who was learning. Chaisson continued to train, taking advantage of resources in the city that were not readily available in small town Newfoundland. Just answering questions from Michael's parents, one of whom was a doctor, required copious amounts of research about autism.

She spoke at length with other professionals working in the field of autism, absorbing what she could from them. She worked with Michael in a daycare environment and took advantage of Calgary's autism resource facilities. Eventually she grew confident that much of what the big city could offer children on the autism spectrum was perfectly achievable, albeit on a smaller scale, in rural Newfoundland.

Despite that belief it wasn't her intention to co-found a group for parents.

Upon her return to Port-aux-Basques in September 2012 she resumed working privately with the little boy she'd left before her move, resuming her strong friendship with the family, which is how she came to be listening to this mother's concerns one afternoon.

This wasn't the first time the mother had told Chaisson how she felt about the challenges of caring for a child on the autism spectrum. By now these chats between the two women had become almost part of their daily routine.

In Newfoundland and Labrador 1 in 57 children are diagnosed as on the Autism Spectrum Disorder (ASD)[1], which is higher than the Canadian national average of 1 in 66.

Simple tasks that most families take for granted, like dining out or going to the doctor's office, were logistical nightmares that left the young mother feeling exasperated.

Both women knew that there were other children in town on the spectrum, and it was likely that their parents and caregivers were also experiencing similar challenges and frustrations.

The two wondered if other parents or caregivers would come to a meeting to chat about their private struggles and frustrations. After discussing the possibility, the women decided to write a post on social media to investigate if there was any interest in forming a support group.

Like many smaller communities in the region, a lot of local events or activities are posted on a town's unofficial Facebook forum page. On January 27, 2013 four people showed up to the first support meeting for parents of children on the autism spectrum, and Autism Involves Me (AIM) was up and running.

Under the mother's guidance, parents were soon able to meet regularly to share experiences, challenges and offer solutions as well as gain support and learn from others. The experiences they shared were varied and prompted by the parents themselves.

---

[1] Autism Spectrum Disorders Among Children and Youth in Canada 2018: A report of the National Autism Spectrum Disorder Surveillance System – *The Public Health Agency of Canada, March 2018.*

Emotional and practical support for local families dealing with the daily frustration of living with autism was initially the group's only real goal and remained its key focus for the first few years.

Parents not only shared their own experiences, but also learned through prepared workshops about such things as dietary needs and sensory needs, or how to recognize the differences between a tantrum and a full meltdown.

Some of the group's meetings offered practical solutions, like how to help their children develop more gross motor skills before they stepped into a school environment that involved physical education classes.

With her background and resources, Chaisson would research for possible solutions to the parents' challenges, offer tips and discuss any frustrations that may occur in public environments and share new books and resources at each meeting.

Members of the group also kept records of the struggles they encountered whenever venturing outside the home with their children, and the notes helped shape future workshops.

Caregivers who had felt alone and overwhelmed were now coming together in a safe and confidential space to build friendships and support networks. In Chaisson, they were also benefiting from a retired educator with a significant amount of training, creative thinking and practical experience to help them develop practical solutions.

"I did not have any children of my own who had autism, but I learned to listen to parents when they were talking about their experiences and challenges," says Chaisson. "I had the time, energy and ability to meet with people, work together as a team and I learned to accept criticism."

The group continued to gain traction as grandparents, educators and resource workers began coming to the meetings. They created their own Facebook group to exchange toys and resources, offer advice and support, celebrate milestones, upload photos and keep each other up to date with the progress they were making. Like parents everywhere, they just wanted their children to grow up safe and happy and they were willing to do whatever it took to make that happen.

There was no intention to build a community model for other towns or community groups to emulate.

"It was just to have a community where our children would be happy living," says Chaisson. "This has grown into something much more."

This small group of caregivers, educators and resource workers were not only about to change their own lives and that of their children, but also change the region itself to such an extent that even the rest of Canada noticed.

CHAPTER TWO
Change, compromise and caregivers

It's not always easy to pack up and leave your home, even if it does appear to be the best route for your child's future. Like most parents, Joanie Sheppard's priority has always been her child. Her son, Christopher, is eight.

Traveling from their home in South Branch to Channel-Port aux Basques was time consuming, taking about a half hour each way. It was also highly inconvenient as she didn't have her own car or any real way to get back and forth, meaning she had to rely on others for a ride since there's no public transit from the Codroy Valley to the regional hub.

Sheppard's biggest motivation for relocating was that Christopher would grow up isolated not just geographically, but socially and emotionally as well.

"He never really had any friends, nowhere to go," recalls Sheppard. "Since we moved down here he's had more things to do, more places to go."

Sheppard became involved with Autism Involves Me in 2015, shortly after Christopher was officially diagnosed. Although she knew something was going on with her son, she wasn't sure what it was.

Five years later she says she's still learning and so is Christopher. Now he participates in a variety of activities including skating, swimming and bowling. For Joanie the move has meant that in addition to help from her relatives, she now enjoys peer support via the AIM group meetings.

"He's just happy. His social skills and everything have improved," she smiles, adding that her son has friends now. "A lot of his skills have improved."

For Kayla MacDonald the decision to pull up stakes took a bit more consideration and effort.

Initially MacDonald had little thought of leaving Hamilton, Ontario. She ran a small pet grooming business from her home and Koston, whose initial diagnosis at age two listed him as being on a more severe level, was now four and responding well to intensive therapy.

"Koston began to not only thrive but started talking and getting better with his motor skills. This was huge! We realized how much therapy and hard work on our end was helping shape our little boy to become the best he could be," recalls MacDonald.

That hard work and therapy was put at risk once the Ontario provincial government, under Doug Ford, began to scale back funding and resources to families of children with ASD. Like many other parents and caregivers at the time, MacDonald found the changes confusing and stressful.

"When the plan came into place the decision was to change therapy based off of age, instead of needs based," says MacDonald. "I still don't understand exactly how they were trying to help our kids but basically many families got no funding at all or were put back on a wait list to get it. And how it worked was kids under the age of 5, once their name came up to the top of the list they would get $20,000 worth of funding for the year and kids 6 and older only get $5,000 a year. But like I said, many families got nothing at all and are still waiting."

The effect on Koston was noticeable. MacDonald was lucky enough to get funding but it was nowhere near enough to cover what her son needed. The new budget model meant he would receive enough money to pay for only two to four hours a week to cover both speech and ABA therapy.

"Before cutbacks Koston was offered what he needed but wait lists were long so we actually didn't get into the Ontario autism program for about a year after applying. And when Koston's name came up on the list they paused the process to come up with their new plan. For a lot of families with children, being diagnosed at an older age meant they had waited years on the list," said MacDonald. "With the wait and having no therapy for that time, we saw Koston's progress slow down. We then knew how important early intervention and needs-based therapy was. It's so detrimental for these children's futures."

She and her partner re-evaluated their situation and came to the conclusion that in order to do what was best for Koston, they would likely have to leave Ontario. MacDonald began researching what other provinces were offering for children with autism and found a video highlighting how Channel-Port aux Basques had been declared the most autism-friendly town in Canada. It certainly helped that MacDonald already had ties to the area.

"I am familiar with Port-aux-Basques because I have close family that lives there and spent almost every childhood summer in the town visiting family and friends. After doing more research about Port-aux-Basques and its dedication to autism, we knew this was going to be our future home. We just had a lot to figure out in terms of leaving our life behind here in Ontario and making the move out there."

MacDonald reached out to Chaisson, who answered her questions and put her in touch with provincial colleagues who helped further clarify what kind of resources Koston would have available. In the end,

MacDonald says it turned out to be a relatively easy decision, although the move itself took around six months to complete.

Koston now has access to the resources while MacDonald grooms small pets from her new shop.

"My favorite part is how the community has completely adapted to these kids and go above and beyond to ensure they not only feel accepted and respected, but educate them to not feel ashamed of having the disability. They teach them that what they have is actually an ability, which in return leaves them to believe they are like little superheros. I can't even express how much that warms my heart. I never have heard of another community going so above and beyond. It truly is spectacular."

Another parent who can testify to the positive impact AIM's resources have had on his child is Michael Patey.

Patey says his son, Connor, was only a couple of years old when he was diagnosed and recalls that hearing his son had autism was a bit of a shock at first. Now eight, Connor has developed into a happy-go-lucky child.

Connor is non-verbal but Patey believes that taking advantage of the town's resources has made a difference for his son. He credits the sensory gym and sports programs offered at the Bruce II Sports Centre as having a tremendous positive impact on Connor.

"He loves the water. He has no fear of water, which is a big fear of mine," says Patey, as he watches over his son who is playing nearby. Having the opportunity to take his son to such an affordable, safe facility helps bring Connor out of his shell and that makes Patey happy too.

It's also the socialization in swimming and bowling that has made a difference for Connor. When Patey used to take his son to the park to play, Connor would quickly retreat into the car and refuse. Now that Connor's social skills have improved, the pair will meet up with another parent whose child is on the spectrum for scheduled play dates.

Connor's favourite park is Andy's Rainbow Park which has a large wooden train for children to climb in or over. Shortly after Connor's diagnosis, Patey made a financial contribution to its construction. A wooden train that children can clamber around in may sound unassuming but Patey is adamant on its importance to his son's overall development.

Connor can't regularly avail of all resources AIM has in place. He lives outside the region in a smaller coastal community with his mother, and it's only when he visits his father that he is able to enjoy them. Patey says when his child has access to these resources, he sees a huge difference in his son, who usually does not adapt well to change.

Even the education system in some of the smaller communities aren't usually equipped to handle children on the autism spectrum or with developmental challenges. Patey says that after his ex-partner relocated, Connor had to miss the first week of the smaller school because they didn't have proper resources in place to help him.

He worries about his son's future without easy access to these resources. The need to have such access also has proven to pay dividends for families almost immediately, not just in the child's future.

Terry Harvey is a talented local musician and former nurse who volunteers his time playing acoustic guitar in the AIM resource room. His wife, Veronica, is a retired teacher and one of Joan Chaisson's former colleagues and friends.

One of AIM's first fundraising efforts was a variety musical show. Tickets were sold at the door and musicians volunteered their time and talents.

After some gentle coaxing by his wife, Harvey performed as one of the musical acts. Later on, the two women thought it might be nice for the children to enjoy a bit of music during Thursday social play dates.

"Again, I got volunteered," he laughs. "I got down there and I started singing songs. And that's when I ran into my first problem."

Children with ASD tend not to provide any immediate feedback that a longtime musical performer might come to expect, like applause or cheers. Harvey felt like he was being ignored and unsure if the kids were actually enjoying his efforts or if he might be annoying them.

Harvey had performed for children before. The kids usually sat in a semi-circle to watch while he played and clapped or sang along, at least until they got bored. But at the AIM play dates he says he felt utterly disconnected.

Chaisson encouraged Harvey to stick with it, telling him that autistic children perceived the world differently and through their own filters. She assured him that the kids were listening and that eventually it would become apparent.

Her advice proved prophetic. Harvey recalls clearly the first afternoon he was strumming and singing a children's song, and stopped mid-verse. One of the children immediately piped in to finish the song and he realized that they were listening quite intently even as they played with their toys or drew pictures.

"It was kind of hard on the ego at first," he admits with a soft laugh.

Harvey admits it was an eye-opening lesson but it has made a difference in how he now perceives the importance of his time spent playing for the group. He loves going to the sessions and his efforts to connect with the children through music have proven successful. If he sits on the floor with the children they will now come over and engage with him more often.

Despite his medical background and the fact that he has a grandchild on the spectrum, Harvey says he has learned a great deal about autism that he did not know before. His grandson enjoys playing with Legos and Harvey will sit and help him build, but once the boy becomes frustrated he throws the bricks down and will stomp away. This used to confuse Harvey who couldn't understand why his grandson would invite him to play only to get upset and leave soon after.

Learning that his grandchild perceived things differently allowed Harvey to adapt. Instead of trying to help his grandson build, Harvey simply sat next to the child and left him alone to build his own Lego tower. After a while, instead of rushing off, his grandson enthusiastically brought Harvey into his world by commenting about the tower.

"That's when it really clicked in," grins Harvey. "I understand this now. This is what I've been learning all along."

Harvey learned that he didn't have to instruct his grandson on how to play, or even play with the same toy, but simply be nearby and available in order to forge a loving, crucial bond.

The musician says there are others in his family on the autism spectrum, including two nephews. One is now an adult who has completed post-secondary studies in computer science.

While his nephew's future seems secure, Harvey still worries as he watches all of the children he's encountered grow into adulthood, wondering how they will fit into a society that expects conformity.

"Our society is basically, 'This is society. You have to fit in,'" he says. "How can we help them adjust to what we're doing? How can we adjust to what they're doing?"

Harvey points out that even foreign immigrants from different socio-economic backgrounds and religions who choose to move to Newfoundland and Labrador are expected to conform readily and easily to a culture and environment they've usually never before experienced.

Harvey believes society itself must become more flexible, although he is keenly aware of just how slowly society moves when it comes to acceptance.

"What is the worst thing you can do with someone who is different? You separate them."

He points out that for many years there were separate Protestant and Catholic school boards in the towns of the province. Once the school boards amalgamated, the two groups learned to put their differences aside and come together to better their schools for the children.

"You have to look out for each other."

CHAPTER THREE
Benefit by helping

Charities and other community groups operating primarily in a rural setting face some extra challenges, but they do have at least one crucial advantage – people know each other. With that knowledge usually comes trust, which means a door is more likely to be opened when asking for help.

In an urban setting like St. John's, there is a larger population to draw upon, and it's easier to knock off a few city blocks in an hour or two when soliciting are door to door. In rural communities, homes tend to be spread out more, so time and travel must also be considered.

The Southwest Coast of Newfoundland, where Autism Involves Me operates, is comprised of small towns, local service districts and everything in between. The Codroy Valley region alone boasts 15 distinct communities.

Geographically, the region is usually considered by locals to extend from South Branch to Rose Blanche-Harbour Le Cou, which is over a ninety minute drive in good weather conditions.

Visitors that arrive to the province via the Marine Atlantic ferry disembark in Channel-Port aux Basques, which is the largest town in the immediate vicinity and serves as the economic and regional hub. Nestled at the far western edge of the Trans Canada Highway, the town's 4000 or so residents form the largest part of the region's 8,500+ populace.[2]

As the main road winds its way through downtown, shuttered and faded commercial buildings often juxtapose with busy adjacent shops. A lot of local commerce occurs at the single mall in Grand Bay, which homes one of the town's two grocery stores and a couple of the larger retailers. There is a health care centre and doctors with private practices, but any specialized medical care or testing is a minimum two-hour drive away.

There's a slower pace of life here that the residents truly embrace and enjoy. There are no traffic lights because they're not necessary, and all year round many people will eschew driving just because it's a beautiful day for a walk.

Even if they don't know each other all that well, they certainly recognize each other's faces or surnames. They do for each other as they have always done, because that is how small towns tend to work.

During those first couple of years, while the support group found its footing and began humming along, Joan Chaisson found herself stepping into the role of resouce co-ordinator.

She gathered more and more resources for parents and children to use, particularly books and toys she had collected for her own classrooms and private students throughout the years.

It soon became apparent that AIM needed somewhere secure to store the growing list of resources and ideally offer a safe space for caregivers and children in need of a break.

It wasn't a small favour to ask.

---

[2] Statistics Canada Census Profile, 2016.

Some of the group's resources are limited and costly, like the weighted sensory vests and blankets. Weighted items have extra materials embedded within during manufacture to provide additional weight which can help soothe and calm a child by providing deep touch pressure.

"A sensory vest is $750," notes Chaisson.

The blankets and vests needed to be kept secure when they weren't being loaned out to families for short periods of time for evaluation or on an as-needed basis. After testing these items first, parents than can decide if it's worth the cost of purchasing one privately.

Regardless of cost, all of AIM's resources needed to be kept in a secure but easily accessible space. But there were also hidden costs to consider such as public liability.

AIM was a fledgling volunteer group without a business number or charitable status and no real way to pay for rental space. Enticing someone to offer a room for free without any perceivable immediate benefit seemed like a long shot.

"Money is the bottom line for any business," says Chaisson.

Still, the group had nothing to lose and everything to gain.

Chaisson sent out a query on social media and almost immediately entrepreneurs Jeannette and Shawn Tobin answered the call.

The Tobins own and operate First Choice Convenience and its entire building, parts of which they sublet. The convenience store itself is flanked by businesses on both sides, and has a basement apartment overlooking the ocean, which is accessible only around the back. Jeanette realized that adjacent to the apartment she had an empty storage space that might work for AIM's needs.

"I'm doing it for the kids," says Tobin. "Kids are everything. They didn't have anywhere for their reading materials and it brings a smile to my face knowing I could just do something."

Tobin doesn't necessarily subscribe to the small town community spirit factor. Even in a big city environment, she believes that the only trick to find a willing business partner to step forward is finding the right person who really cares and is in a position to offer help.

In Tobin's case, that help involves very little money. She pays for the heat, but since the room is only used as needed, it's a minor expense. She has allowed the group to decorate and furnish the room as they see fit, even offering some extra paint she had in storage. Tobin says any group that asked might have availed of the space but until AIM actually did she hadn't thought to offer the room.

What was once a dull, forgotten industrial storage space is now a bright, colourful room lined with shelves laden with toys and books, while nearby comfy chairs offer a quiet corner. Adorning the walls are bright murals, a labour of love painted by local artist Alex LeRiche, who has repeatedly volunteered his time and talents.

There's a small table with a coffee pot for when parents need a break and a chat, and a large table in the centre of the room to conduct regular meetings or that the children use to play games or craft during the social play dates.

The resources are checked in and out, similar to a library. Children can check out any of the materials, allowing parents to decide whether or not its worthwhile to make the investment for their child.

AIM keeps its own hours and its own set of keys with full autonomy to use the space as the group sees fit.

Upstairs in her store, Tobin keeps a little cup for AIM by the cash register and hands the donations over to the group every time it gets full. It might only be $10 or so, but it all adds up and eventually results in another resource brought into the room for the children.

Most importantly, what Tobin and her staff offer is a safe space for children and caregivers, a place to house resources, but most importantly just to socialize and share experiences. There's a practicality to helping out that is undeniable. As these children grow into teenagers and eventual adulthood, they will continue to form some of the convenience store's clientele.

A key part of AIM's work with the children involves developing practical life skills. The kids come into the convenience store and make their own purchases. They are taught to take their treats to the counter, count out the correct amount of money, receive any proper change and interact with the staff.

These everyday transactions that most people take for granted are often monumental milestones for some of the children on the autism spectrum.

"They weren't used to it," admits Tobin.

Initially the children would come into the shop and just run around. In just a few short years the change Tobin has witnessed firsthand has been remarkable.

"They'll say hi and they'll ask for what they want, and it's awesome. I can't believe the difference in them."

One little boy in particular stands out for Tobin. He always comes in wearing a furry hat and initially was very hyper, running through the aisles. Now he walks in and exchanges pleasantries with her and discusses his time at school before asking for whatever it is he wants to purchase.

Tobin doesn't believe that such significant change would have happened, at least not as easily, without the work of the AIM volunteers who took the time to train both the children and the store's staff.

"The schools around here are good but there's not enough one-on-one," offers Tobin.

If the store's profile has risen or benefited at all from its owner's philanthropy, Tobin is either unaware of it or dismisses it outright. In fact, when CBC News came to town to document some of AIM's work, Tobin declined to be interviewed.

"I'm not doing it for the business part of it," says Tobin. "I don't want recognition for it. I'm doing it for the kids. Just as long as I know it's helping out a kid or helping out somebody, that's all I need."

If Tobin is nonchalant about cost and benefits for her store, that is not always possible for other business owners or managers.

In order to help the children develop those crucial gross motor skills what AIM really wanted was a place to create a sensory gym. The resource room beneath the store wasn't nearly big enough, which meant another location had to be found.

The Bruce II Sports Centre is a regional sports and recreational facility located in the Grand Bay area of town, in close proximity to a daycare and both the elementary and high schools. It boasts a swimming pool, bowling alley, skating and hockey rink, curling ice, walking track, gym equipment, a café and several meeting rooms.

The arena is operated by the town council and as such must remain fiscally responsible to taxpayers. Sensory equipment can be expensive and it was unrealistic to believe that the council or the arena's management could cover those costs, no matter how willing they might be to help.

Prior to asking for a meeting, Chaisson drafted a presentation detailing what equipment AIM wanted to install and how the arena itself would benefit just by offering them some gym space.

At the crux of AIM's presentation was the argument that bringing in sensory equipment would not only help make the facility more accessible for children with autism, but would make it more accessible for all children in the region. Researching the equipment the group wanted to install was key.

"We decided what we needed to buy and found out the total cost. Then we researched grants that were available," says Chaisson.

In this case, AIM researched provincial and federal grants available for autism, healthy living and integration that might offset some of the cost of the equipment purchase. It was clear they would also have to develop strategies to fundraise.

"We explained how we needed their space, their insurance policy and that they would be in charge of cleaning and organizing the use of the equipment," recalls Chaisson.

Wanda Ryan Merrigan was active with the Bruce II for years prior to becoming the facility's manager. While there were local children on the spectrum able to participate in hockey or figure skating classes, it wasn't always suitable for some of the others.

"They were looking for a way to have sort of structured and non-structured play for the kids where they could be physically active," says Merrigan. "That's what started it all."

The timing couldn't have been better. Only weeks prior to the meeting with Chaisson, Merrigan had completed a fundamental movement skills training course through Recreation Newfoundland and Labrador. (RNL).

While the Bruce II was already well-equipped to offer programs for school age children, those with developmental challenges or preschool children required a different approach. Feeling somewhat restricted by what the arena had to offer, Merrigan had signed on to the training course, which would dovetail perfectly with what AIM was trying to offer.

"Because of technology nowadays, they say young children are not learning the skills that we learned," explains Merrigan. "Running, hopping, skipping, jumping, throwing – that type of thing."

Merrigan knew there were some initial hurdles that would have to be overcome. In addition to financing, unlike the convenience store, the arena didn't have an extra, unused room it could offer.

The sensory gym equipment at the Bruce II Sports Centre is designed to be easily disassembled to be stored out of sight when not in use. The equipment, which is available to all children visiting the facility, is free for children with ASD while the rest of the general public pay a nominal fee to help offset maintenance costs.

Merrigan brought the issue to the Recreation Committee, a committee comprised of facility employees, council members and town employees. Under the approval of Town Council, it was decided that a heavy curtain could be pulled across the far end of the walking track during specific times to serve as a sensory friendly gymnasium. A large storage area behind the far wall would allow the sensory equipment to be stored close by for easy access when not in use.

Children affiliated with AIM would use the equipment during private sessions at no charge. In return, twice a week the Bruce II would offer a drop-in playtime for all preschool children for a small fee of $3 per child. That fee would help offset the cost of arena staff who would have to clean, set up the equipment and place it all back into storage between sessions. The Bruce II would also be able to use the equipment to rent out the space for birthday parties for children from ages 1 through 5.

Within a year the sensory gym was officially opened. The equipment wasn't cheap but AIM and the Bruce II had benefited from a major donation by the Canadian Tire Jumpstart program, along with smaller donations from local businesses, organizations and parents.

Merrigan says there are plenty of preschool children not on the spectrum who visit regularly to socialize and play. The equipment appeals to children regardless of any sensory issues, and just being active helps all of them to develop. Merrigan says the kids don't know or care about the difference – they're just happy to play.

"Most of the equipment we have in there is sensory equipment," says Merrigan. "It's a balance beam you can walk on, but it's a textured balance beam. So all kids can use a balance beam, but the kids who are on the spectrum like the textured portion of it."

Although it may have started with a small gym to develop motor skills, together the Bruce II and AIM have found even more ways for the facility to become truly autism friendly.

Almost half of accidental injuries or deaths for individuals with autism (46 per cent) occur by drowning. In particular, children on the spectrum, between ages five and seven, drown 160 times more frequently than their neurotypically developing peers.[3]

It's a sobering, brutal statistic.

Children who wander, particularly at night when their parents are sleeping, can be drawn to water as a pleasing visual stimulus. Living in an oceanside community or a region littered with ponds makes this is a very real hazard.

With that in mind, staff at the Bruce II and AIM developed new strategies for both group and private lessons as the facility's regular group lessons aren't always practical. At times even Merrigan has found it too loud to focus with so many children splashing around in the pool.

"We have children on the spectrum who take part in our regular swimming lessons, but if you have a child who has auditory sensory issues, the hearing is magnified," says Merrigan. "Everything down there is amplified. It's concrete walls and water. What better conductors of sound?"

Some children with hearing sensitivities who attempted to participate in the group sessions couldn't even make it into the change rooms before having a meltdown. The private lesson structure also needed tweaking.

"Even in a private lesson, we might have eight or nine sessions on the go at one time, which means you have eight or nine children with eight or nine instructors, and their parents and siblings," says Merrigan.

The AIM program sessions permit only three instructors and three children in the pool at any one time. Each year, before the children begin their lessons, the instructors , mostly high school students who are also lifeguards, must undergo additional training.

"In the beginning, we had to do a little bit of research on how to adapt some of our lessons, because if you have a child who is non-verbal, the way you're going to teach a child who is non-verbal is different than

---

[3] Injury Mortality in Individuals With Autism – *Columbia Centre for Injury Epidemiology and Prevention,* *June 2017.*

the way you're going to teach a child who can talk back to you," says Merrigan.

The lifeguards are carefully selected. Merrigan chooses instructors who can adapt quickly to the unexpected, are naturally patient, and will likely succeed through trial and error rather than just feeling frustrated.

The first three high school students she picked would go on to serve as models for all instructors who followed. In between their own classes and other commitments, the three lifeguards spent time conducting their own research and offering valuable feedback to other Bruce II swim staff and AIM.

"It didn't surprise me, because that's the type of young ladies they were," offers Merrigan.

If Merrigan has any regrets, it's that those first three instructors are no longer lifeguards at the Bruce II. They have all moved on to university, where she fully expects they will continue to excel. Constantly training new lifeguards is simply part of the ongoing process.

Of course those lessons must come with a cost. The lifeguards are trained employees, not volunteers, as are all staff at the Bruce II. But the facility is not looking to turn a profit or render the lessons too expensive and out of reach for families.

"We do AIM's private lessons at the same rate as what we charge other children for group," says Merrigan. "We charge enough to cover off our instructor expenses."

While finances will always remain a consideration for the facility, Merrigan says she hasn't seen any real extra costs for the Bruce II.

If anything, installing the sensory gym and developing the swim program has only proven to benefit the arena by making it more attractive and accessible for regional families and even tourists who visit the area.

Whatever training the staff and volunteers have undergone has always been free, whether it is delivered through the Autism Society of Newfoundland and Labrador or through AIM.

The training and hard work has done exactly what AIM and the Bruce II intended. Merrigan has witnessed the benefits children have reaped from these crucial lessons.

For example, a five year old boy repeatedly rejected attempts to get him to shed his life jacket. At some point he grew brave enough to put his face and then his whole head into the water. Eventually he decided he was ready and wanted to jump into the water from the diving blocks along the deep end of the pool.

Merrigan grabbed her phone and began filming, knowing full well his parents would never believe her otherwise. He hesitated at least a half dozen times, always advising Merrigan when she could start filming again, and in front of a room full of lifeguards he finally jumped in. When he broke the surface again, Merrigan says his smile lit up the whole building. His love of the water combined with his newfound confidence soon made him unstoppable.

"Every child needs to be good at something. For a lot of children who on the spectrum, their peers are good at hockey or riding their bike or they're good at figure skating – all kinds of different things. So to be really good at something – every child needs that."

And then there are the hidden, unexpected benefits. One of the lifeguards received a significant university scholarship thanks in part to her work with the AIM swim program.

Meanwhile Merrigan finds herself giving interviews to peers in places like New York and fielding phone calls from foreign countries about how to implement similar programs elsewhere.

She says the goal is increasing accessibility, not only for children on the autism spectrum, but for all of the facility's patrons, while keeping extra costs at a minimum for families. The positive, determined attitude of the arena's staff is another key factor.

Merrigan fully believes that other facilities can follow suit for all people with disabilities or challenges.

"I think the biggest thing you need to do is the education piece," offers Merrigan, but even that advice comes with a caveat. "I think you do it little bit by little bit. You pick away at it."

It's sound advice. Educating large groups on how to train an autistic child to swim can be outright overwhelming and Merrigan says the smaller scale approach is much easier to manage. The Bruce II and AIM continue to maintain this approach simply because it has proven so effective.

By necessity Merrigan became a de facto authority on developing specialized sports programs and has been recruited to train other facility managers at RNL meetings.

The first presentation she did, roughly six years ago, was scheduled to be a 15-minute slideshow presentation about the Bruce II's partnership with AIM on developing the sensory gym. It ran longer than 50 minutes because of the numerous questions, not only from towns with similar recreation facilities, but from volunteer staff of smaller outport communities who had never before considered installing a sensory gym or developing a dedicated resource room in an unused space.

Perhaps most importantly, Merrigan has become highly familiar with what federal, provincial and private grants are available to offset equipment or training costs. GoodLife Fitness, for example, has a charitable grant that the Bruce II Sports Centre has received to further develop programs.

"I chair the local chapter of Canadian Tire Jumpstart," notes Merrigan, who had been in that role long before AIM was even founded. "We've gotten money from local groups such as the Lions Club and provincial funding. There are different types of funding you can get. We got funding from Easter Seals. We bought a sledge."

The hockey sledge is also available during general skating as well, and after that first sledge the facility, in partnership with AIM, received grants to buy more sledges that all of the Bruce II arena patrons can use, not just those on the autism spectrum.

"We don't have enough children to make a sledge hockey league, but children who have mobility issues, and there are children on the spectrum whose coordination is not good enough to skate, they can ride a sledge."

Merrigan says the sledges cost about twelve hundred dollars each and that help with funding came from a provincial inclusivity grant and GoodLife Kids Foundation.

"The whole idea is to help these children fit into their community and be able to participate rather than have to sit on the sidelines."

The Bruce II Sports Centre and AIM eventually acquired 11 sledges. Details surrounding rentals have yet to be finalized but so far the sledges are proving to be a hit with everyone who has tried them.

Including children on the spectrum has also affected the arena's other programs that were already well established and initially not designed to accommodate them. They can now enjoy Friday bowling sessions, and children can even spend an entire day at the facility with trained staff who know how to accommodate their needs.

About eight years ago a child on the spectrum joined the Summer Sports program, which is a child sports day camp that the Bruce II has offered for many years. Merrigan recalls that it was incredibly stressful for everyone.

"We had no knowledge or skills so we didn't know how to respond or react. We were constantly in contact with the parent and the parents were having to come over. It wasn't fun, and it wasn't fun for the other kids," she admits.

About three years ago that program began to change for the better too. There's now a training plan in place to help accommodate children with sensory sensitivities.

Initially Joan Chaisson first meets with the group to give a presentation on autism. Next, parents of the children meet with the program counselors to discuss what works best for their child. It's not a long or difficult meeting, but a simple step that informs the counselors and allows them to interact positively with their young charges, who in turn enjoy coming to camp rather than feeling stressed.

Another hidden but important benefit is that their neurotypical peers also learn from a young age how to play with others who are facing developmental or physical challenges, so play is now much more fun and inclusive for all. Merrigan has even witnessed some children ask friends on the spectrum if they need a sensory break, then help them break when it's needed or inform a counselor.

"The kids know, the children all know. It's not hidden anymore. One time people wouldn't talk about it and people wouldn't declare it on their registration forms," says Merrigan. "Instead of them getting angry, you see the child stop."

When first rolling out the new Summer Sports program, the Bruce II secured additional funding for a dedicated counselor for children on the autism spectrum, and all of the camp's children knew her role and who they could turn to for extra help.

"It worked like a charm," says Merrigan.

It worked so well, in fact, that they hired the counselor back for a second summer, and subsequently all of the program counselors are now equipped to handle meltdowns and sensory issues.

"It's a completely different environment here now. Four or five years ago we had children register and we were like, 'How are we going to handle them because they don't listen?' Now we know why. Now it's a run of the mill thing here. Now if a kid has a meltdown here, it's just like another one has peed their pants."

Merrigan says the driving force that has made the Bruce II more accessible is AIM and Joan Chaisson, who simply doesn't take no for an answer.

"If she asks you something, she's not asking you and waiting for you to say yes or no," chuckles Merrigan. "When you start to respond she assumes it's a yes and she's carrying on with it."

Regardless of any financial benefit for the sports facility through increased usage, much of Merrigan's motivation and effort to make the Bruce II Sports Centre more accessible and accepting seems to stem from the exactly the same place as Jeannette Tobin's.

"It just warms my heart."

Unfortunately not every community has a regional sports centre to approach for help. Chaisson advises other groups with strict financial budgets to first look for a public partner. Even the smallest community usually has a public building with proper liability insurance.

Partnering with the community itself is always vital when it comes to promoting awareness, educating residents and fundraising. She suggests a similar approach is also effective for larger urban areas.

"I urge them to work in small communities in their city," offers Chaisson. "Then they can expand into the next neighbourhood. Sometimes it can be overwhelming to try to change the whole city at once."

CHAPTER FOUR
Canada's first autism-friendly hotel

While members of Autism Involves Me were still busy setting up the resource room and working with the Bruce II, they also began a steady campaign to educate the public and raise community awareness.

It didn't take long before AIM meetings were now drawing healthcare professionals, educators and business owners interested in learning more about increasing accessibility. One local business even began paying for a space in the newspaper that offered a short educational fact about autism to help raise awareness.

Volunteers with AIM participated in community parades and appeared regularly at community events and celebrations. Even the parades themselves became autism friendly. Flashing lights and loud sirens are now shut off during one portion of the route so that citizens with sensory sensitivities can enjoy the floats.

As the AIM meetings continued, a new challenge emerged. Parents of children on the autism spectrum were finding it difficult, if not outright impossible, to dine out, vacation or just relax.

Many had resorted to eating and sleeping in their vehicles when needing to travel because their vehicles provided a safe, soothing and familiar space for their child.

Chaisson did some research and discovered an autism friendly hotel in Florida, which had made changes to accommodate its owner's son who was on the spectrum. Armed with this knowledge, she readied her pitch and scheduled a meeting with the owner of Hotel Port aux Basques.

Nestled near the town's train museum and overlooking the Trans Canada Highway, the two-story structure does its best to promote traditional Newfoundland and Labrador culture and local cuisine. An enormous stuffed moose head adorns the one wall of the lobby and a cozy fireplace flanked by comfortable lounge chairs offers a warm welcome just opposite the main door.

While AIM had suggestions on how to make renovations to the bedrooms and restaurant, the group were also seeking an additional space to install a sensory room. This calming room would provide hotel guests and local children with a dedicated, accessible space to take sensory breaks.

Owner Cathy Lomond signed on for the challenge without hesitation. Lomond has a sister with Down's Syndrome whom she helped raise since childhood, and knew firsthand the difficulties facing families of children with special needs.

Developing a strategic plan, completing the changes and educating staff evolved into a two-year joint effort between AIM and Hotel Port aux Basques.

Consultations with local parents revealed that one of their biggest issues when traveling was safety. They were worried that children could break or throw items in the rooms. In addition, many children have a tendency to wander, especially at night. In order for a parent or caregiver to get any real rest, they'd have to feel confident the child would not be able to exit the room unnoticed.

"It's not rocket science. Sometimes you feel, 'My God, this is so easy. How come we never did it before?'" Lomond asks rhetorically. "You know it cost me 12 grand just to put a few tables and chairs in my bar. It didn't cost me a thousand dollars – I don't know if it even cost me five hundred dollars – to do 16 rooms that are autism friendly because it's so easy."

Lomond says that hoteliers who contact her for advice typically just want to know where to start. She tells them to head to their nearest dollar store and buy some childproof drawer sliders.

Once they know that a guest requires an autism friendly room, Lomond's staff prepares the suite by placing coffee pots, phone books and other items into the safety drawers.

"It's the same ones you'd put on your drawers at home if you had an infant," she says.

She also advises hoteliers to head to the local hardware store to buy some old-fashioned chain slide locks and install them as high as possible inside the door, out of reach of young hands. Once the child can't walk out or access anything breakable or easily thrown, the parents feel that they can actually relax and enjoy their stay.

"When you go to bed you want to be able to sleep just like every other parent," says Lomond. "When you're in a hotel, which is a foreign environment for them, it's more stress for the parents and it's more stress on the child who is autistic."

Usually hotels bolt all televisions and artwork to the wall securely as a matter of course to deter theft or damage. Lomond simply upgraded or replaced any substandard bolts.

The next step was overhauling her restaurant's menu. Guided by AIM, Lomond learned that a lot of autistic children are non-verbal and have food sensitivities. Using an in-house printer and working with her chef, Lomond designed a kid friendly picture menu. *(see page 95)*

Children can simply point to the item they want instead of a parent having to read it to them or try to force a choice, and the food will always be presented exactly as it appears in the photo. That means if ice cream is on the menu in a red bowl it is always served in that exact red bowl and no other.

The menu items are typical kid fare such as a grilled cheese sandwich or French fries. It's offered to every child who stays at the hotel and has proven to be more effective with all children, not just those on the autism spectrum.

In order to ensure that the hotel was indeed fully equipped to handle guests with family members on the spectrum, the Autism Society of Newfoundland and Labrador (ASNL) and AIM conducted training sessions with all front line staff.

Clerks, waitstaff and the chefs have all received the training, and Lomond also invited other local businesses and their staff to attend. Firefighters and town employees were among those who chose to attend the free training.

Lomond recounts a story where an autistic child had a meltdown during dinner, and other diners were heard making remarks that the family should retreat from the restaurant. A server had a discreet word with the other diners, explaining that autistic guests were just as welcome as any other. Once the onlookers realized it wasn't simply a misbehaving child the remarks stopped.

Guests can also request an emailed copy of a slideshow to familiarize their children with the hotel well before they arrive, and are emailed a brief questionnaire regarding their child's needs so that staff will be fully prepared for their arrival.

The slideshow allows a child a virtual walk through the parking lot, lobby, hallways, suite, dining room and sensory room so that they are less overwhelmed by their stay.

"There are so many levels on the spectrum," notes Lomond.

Since the hotel typically decorates for every holiday, sometimes the themes may have to be adjusted. One guest's child was terrified of ghosts, so Lomond had them all removed from the annual Halloween display prior to the family's arrival.

Lomond also allowed AIM to set up the sensory calming room in the basement, just below the hotel's main staircase in an unused employee break room.

The room itself is not large, perhaps 8 by 10 feet, but it represents a safe haven not just for guests but for local children, their parents, and even educators from nearby schools.

Of all the hotel projects, the sensory calming room was the most time consuming but once again did not increase overall operating costs. Lomond simply offered the space and AIM did the rest, procuring items through private donations, provincial and private grants and community fundraising.

"It was of no financial impact to me," says Lomond. "It's amazing how the community came together."

The bland, concrete walls were brightened with colourful murals by local artist Alex LeRiche. One wall has been converted into a rock climbing wall and a large mirror reflects warm light back into the small room. A padded cocoon swing hangs from the ceiling, and sensory toys are stuffed into baskets beneath a bench and throughout the room.

Children can also bring their favourite music to enjoy while they play with the sensory items or enjoy lounging on the pillows or pea pod.

Raising all of the funds for the hotel's sensory room took AIM about a year and the end result has proved enormously popular with all children who visit, not just those on the autism spectrum.

"We need one for adults," laughs Lomond.

Anyone who wishes to use the room is welcome to do so regardless of whether or not they are a hotel guest, but must first sign out the key card

The sensory friendly room at the Hotel Port-aux-Basques is open to all visitors even if they are not guests of the hotel. – © *Courtesy of Hotel Port-aux-Basques*

from the front desk. This not only prevents theft but increases privacy for guests who need a safe space without unexpected interruptions.

The autism friendly hotel model was created entirely by AIM and Hotel Port aux Basques through trial and error, borne of a desire to help parents and families experience something most others do regularly and without hesitation – take a vacation.

Even before the official ribbon cutting ceremony naming it as the first autism friendly hotel in Canada, Lomond was fielding calls from reporters and other hoteliers from a beach in the Caribbean after an article in the town's local newspaper went viral.

Lomond, who has chaired Canada Select's Atlantic Board, has since been working to advise other hotels on how to make similar changes to accommodate their own guests. Some of the accommodation owners Lomond has helped include rental cottage owners at Gros Morne National Park.

Eventually AIM and the Hotel Port aux Basques hope to be able to offer a full retreat weekend package for families who have members on the autism spectrum.

Local businesses have reached out to offer discounts for guests. Some of those incentives will include coupons for haircuts or spa retreats for parents to relax while their children are playing safely at the Bruce II Sports Centre under the supervision of trained caregivers.

The hotel's successful transformation has even prompted a representative from Canada Select to pay a visit to learn more and take reference photos.

"No matter where I go to or travel or meet, they have a family member or friend who has a child with needs. It's so prevalent, more than I ever thought."

While Lomond is unable to determine if the number of guests overall has increased, she has confirmed that people passing through the area will now come to the hotel to dine or use the sensory room simply because they are aware it has autism friendly resources and staff.

For more information on Hotel Port aux Basques and its autism friendly amenities or to make a reservation, visit their website at hotel-port-aux-basques.com.

CHAPTER FIVE
The most autism-friendly town in Canada

Round and square stickers bearing the autism jigsaw puzzle piece logo are easy to spot around Port aux Basques. The words encircling the logo indicates that the business is either autism aware or autism friendly.

Many local businesses have them, including two financial institutions, several restaurants, a grocery chain store and even a church.

This two stage sticker system and business accreditation is another cornerstone in AIM's ongoing efforts to increase acceptance and accessibility.

The first stage of the program certifies a business as autism aware. To qualify, a business owner and/or employees must attend an in-person training session. The sessions are usually scheduled a couple of times a year, once enough businesses have signed on.

This first stage is designed to be a crash course on autism, how it can impact language and communication, and how a customer on the spectrum might process information and react differently during typical transactions. It also offers a general list of constructive ways for businesses to support people on the spectrum, and handouts surrounding facts and myths about autism.

The second stage to certify the business as autism friendly requires an on-site visit for a private consultation between the AIM director and the business.

During the second stage, Chaisson will visit a business and ascertain what if any specific changes it needs to implement to accommodate customers. By then front line staff are expected to have been trained about autism and serving customers on the spectrum, usually by the owner or employee who attended the first session.

Only after AIM is confident that these changes and all training are completed and implemented, will it certify the business as fully autism friendly.

Like almost everything AIM does the stickers form part of a local partnership. In this case, the partner in question is artist Kris Bragg of Kris' Kustoms.

Bragg prints the stickers for free as needed and helps AIM with its fundraising by hosting an annual show and shine car show.

Anyone who brings a vehicle to the show can have its exterior cleaned for free. There's always a party atmosphere surrounding the barbecue, which is hosted by the local Leading Edge Credit Union. After the third year, the event grew to such an extent local school children brought bicycles to be washed and polished while they grabbed a hamburger or a hot dog.

There are no first, second or third prizes given out since both AIM and Bragg promote that each vehicle is unique to its owner, much as children with autism are unique to themselves. In fact, all vehicle owners receive a thank you gift which is made possible by area businesses donating a gift certificate or products.

There is always one large gift, also donated by a local business, which allows AIM to sell tickets as an entry prize. There's also a fifty-fifty draw, where half the proceeds go to the winner and half goes to AIM. Local musicians or a disco operator donate their time and equipment to play music. Every penny raised goes to the AIM group.

Prior to becoming an entrepreneur, Bragg did a stint with the Community Employment Corporation (CEC).

"I worked with several people with autism. Your heart kind of goes out to them, knowing their daily struggles," says Bragg. "It being a small community, everybody knows everyone."

While he admits to having secured some contracts due to the increased exposure, like other business owners who have partnered with AIM, Bragg insists his primary motivation is to help improve accessibility throughout the town.

For now Bragg restricts his charitable partnerships only to AIM. As with most small, independent businesses, money is sometimes tight.

Growing AIM's network has by extension also grown Bragg's own social media profiles both professionally and personally, so his primary contribution is also a non-financial one.

"Events, awareness and social media," says Bragg. "Those are the big three for me."

It's not just small town businesses that are learning too. Even high profile franchises are taking notice.

When it comes to offering autism friendly service, one of the big advantages of a franchise chain is that the furniture, layout, colours, menu and smells tend to be similar no matter which location someone may be visiting.

Peggy McNeil is the owner and operator of the Pizza Delight Restaurant in Port-aux-Basques.

"We have a menu for kids that does have pictures anyway," says McNeil. "That's the Pizza Delight menu."

Her staff have also been fully trained to be autism friendly and are well acquainted with the children who lunch in her restaurant, usually once a week. McNeil believes any business can adapt.

"It was painless for us," shrugs McNeil. "They're no different whatsoever. You get kids that come in and throw tantrums without autism. You learn to deal with it."

Another business which has become autism friendly is the Butterfly Book Boutique. Valerie Parsons is the bookstore owner and is also an elementary school teacher.

Parsons runs book clubs for children and adults, offering an introductory package and a certificate for reading milestones such as number of books. She also carries toys and games in her shop.

Part of her efforts to support AIM includes offering discounts for autism related materials destined for the group's resource room.

"I work with a lot of autistic children and they're all just so wonderful. You learn from them. They inspire you," says Parsons.

Like other business owners that partnered with AIM, she knows most of the kids and their individual personalities and needs. She has also witnessed firsthand the positive changes in her regular patrons, some of who have become increasingly verbal. Not only has she noticed it in the store, she says it also manifests in her classroom and that in turn has allowed children on the spectrum to become increasingly accepted by their peers.

"Every little thing they do, when the communication isn't there, when they grow it's inspiring to me," says Parsons.

She recounts a story about one non-verbal child with a pair of neurotypical children for friends. The trio rushes regularly to Parsons to point out each new milestone the non-verbal child has achieved, and she says the young peer support and acceptance is crucial for development.

Parsons says if she had the space in her shop she'd build a sensory room for the children to retreat to with some of the toys and books she has to offer.

"These children, sometimes they are limited as to where they can go. They want to feel comfortable."

At the St. James Elementary School where she teaches, Parsons has noticed all of the children playing on the new autism friendly equipment that has been installed both in the classrooms and on the playground. Including children on the spectrum does not mean excluding anyone, maintains Parsons. It's just a matter of finding more ways they can participate together.

"Not all populations have a high number of autistic kids, but it doesn't matter if it's four or if it's twenty-four, they still should have the benefits to make them happier and a more productive part of society," says Parsons.

By Spring 2016, AIM's work had become so successful that the group petitioned the Port-aux-Basques town council to declare the town as officially Autism Friendly.

While town council was delighted at the national and international recognition AIM's work had brought to the town, they did insist on a condition before agreeing to sign an official declaration. Specifically, council requested that a reasonable percentage of citizens, based on the town's existing population that did not have children on the spectrum, were going above and beyond to support autism awareness and initiatives.

Chaisson had little trouble finding the required proof.

Even as the business community began to sign on, AIM had been working with first responders, particularly volunteer firefighters, to teach them how to approach a child on the spectrum who might be caught in a hazardous situation. At the same time, AIM focused on raising funds to install autism friendly kits on fire engines. The kits held blankets and various sensory items designed to soothe and calm a child who may be involved in an emergency situation.

Todd Strickland, who served at the time as town mayor, says he was truly honoured to declare Port-aux-Basques as the first Official Autism Friendly Town in Canada on July 19, 2017. Currently a popular and sitting town councilor, he also serves as the Deputy Fire Chief for the town's volunteer fire department.

During his day job, Strickland works as a nurse at the Dr. Charles L. LeGrow Health Centre. He says he has colleagues with children and grandchildren on the spectrum.

Even without the AIM training, he says just listening to people share their stories proved to be a huge education about autism and other disabilities.

"It just got to be almost a daily thing," he says, noting that everyone loves to share stories and anecdotes about their kids and daily life.

As a healthcare professional, he is aware that the town has more kids on the autism spectrum than is statistically normal.

"Because of that it's more out there in the public and you hear about it more often," says Strickland.

When the Newfoundland and Labrador Association of Firefighters (NLAF) partnered with AIM and ASNL to educate firefighters on autism in emergency situations, Strickland found himself learning even more.

"In the time of an emergency it's great to know anything and everything that will help," says Strickland, who believes the training is truly essential.

He attended workshops offered locally and at the provincial fire school, which is also working to grow its awareness training.

Although there was some overlap in the sessions, Strickland says there were plenty of differences which made it beneficial to attend both. He also attended a firefighter convention which offered yet another autism awareness training session.

"That one was really enjoyable because we got into things that we didn't address in the other two," he says.

At the convention, firefighters wore different gear and simulated different sounds so that they could better understand how overwhelming it might appear to a child on the spectrum and how it might cause them to react.

If it seems like a lot of training, Strickland points out that training is a large portion of a firefighter's regular routine anyway as new techniques and technology are constantly being developed and implemented.

"They are doing a really good job of just trying to bring this forward and just make everyone, especially emergency personnel, learn about what autism is," says Strickland. "You can never get enough education."

Strickland says something simple like a puzzle piece sticker in the doorway alerting firefighters that a child on the spectrum is in residence can prove critical in an emergency situation.

"We know that a kid with autism lives there, so we've got to change our strategy on what we're doing and how we're doing it – how we're calling for kids and looking for kids," says Strickland.

He is a firm believer in the importance of the sensory kits AIM donated to all of the region's fire departments. Thankfully they've not yet had to be deployed, but Strickland says the department is fully prepared to do so should it ever prove necessary.

"Most times we say with the fire services not if but when," says Strickland. "We do have a firefighter on our department and one of his kids has autism."

Currently the Channel-Port aux Basques Fire Department has at least three sensory kits equipped on its trucks, with about a dozen similar kits deployed on firetrucks in six other communities along the Southwest Coast.

It's not just firefighters who have received the training either.

Strickland says ambulance attendants, police and social workers also attended the AIM awareness sessions. When it comes to making changes to increase inclusivity, Strickland says he has noticed one thing he finds particularly interesting.

"Not many people ask why."

This flag flying above the town hall in Channel - Port aux Basques signifies its official status as autism friendly. - © *Courtesy of Candace Matthews*

CHAPTER SIX
Sensory friendly schools

It was only a matter of time until parents, educators and members of Autism Involves Me also realized that resources for children needed to be improved at the local schools where they were spending the bulk of their day.

A provincial grant of $3700 allowed AIM to install a new sensory tunnel in the elementary school playground. The tunnel, which all children can use, helps when their senses are overwhelmed during play. They are able to slip into the tunnel for a sensory break, whereas prior to its installation children would retreat inside away from their playmates or even leave school for the day.

The specific tunnel at the town's elementary school was selected by a student who attended and is on the autism spectrum.

During the summer, the school also installed sensory pathways in their upstairs and downstairs corridors. The brightly coloured pathways not only help make the school more fun and welcoming, they allow children to build connections in their brains related to sight, touch and sound. This enables school children to complete complex and multi-stage tasks, and helps with movement breaks and gross motor development.

This sensory tunnel offers a safe, quiet retreat for all of the elementary school's children, not just those on the autism spectrum. – © *Courtesy of J. René Roy*

By promoting physical activity and allowing every student to release some energy, it can help redirect an emotion or behaviour so the child can feel calmness and less anxiety due to a sensory challenge.

Assisted by AIM, the cost of the patterns was procured by a $1,000 donation from the minister of education and $1,000 donation from Western Health.

School custodians installed the pathways by first stripping the wax from the floors and cleaning them thoroughly, then laying the patterns before sealing them with three coats of wax.

Almost directly across the street at the local high school, IR (Instructional Resource) teacher Niki Carroll was working to spearhead some changes as well.

Carroll was convinced that the school needed to build a sensory friendly room for students to retreat to when they needed a break.

There were already a handful of high school students who would benefit, and Carroll was aware that an even greater number of children from the elementary school would soon join the student body when they graduated.

"How do I get this room? Where do I get this money? How do I start?" Carroll recalls asking herself.

The first thing she did was turn to her principal for support, and he jumped on board immediately. She says that without the principal's support any real change is impossible, but although he was on board he had little idea how to proceed. He was sure that the school itself might be able to contribute a bit financially.

Since it was already the winter semester Carroll wanted to ensure the room was completed before summer break and the influx of new students in the fall. The principal suggested Carroll reach out to AIM for help.

One of several sensory paths installed at St. James Elementary School.
© *Courtesy of J. René Roy*

The resulting partnership between the school, AIM and the community itself worked so well that Carroll didn't even bother to petition the school board for funds.

Once again artist Alex LeRiche volunteered his time to spend evenings painting the mural. The entire wall and even the door were transformed into a soothing, colourful depiction of the ferry sailing into the harbour, work that took him well over a month.

The paints and materials were purchased by AIM, and as more funds were raised Chaisson began purchasing necessary sensory equipment including a hammock and pea pod. Carroll also used the school's donations to bring in some smaller supplies and materials. A local business donated a rocking chair and other members of the community volunteered time and supplies.

Once school opened for the fall semester a few students began trickling in. Carroll would like to see more students take advantage of the room, but she's not sure if there's a social stigma involved.

"There's been three that come down now and take advantage," says Carroll. "There's probably a couple more that could, but I think they're just too shy or they don't want their classmates to know."

Although only a handful of students use the room, there are more than 250 students enrolled. All students are granted access, not just those in need of a sensory break. It will be interesting to see how many more come to this room as the school year progresses.

"I had a daughter that received resource support," admits Carroll. "When she first came over for (grades) seven and eight, she was very distraught about going out there because her friends were calling her stupid."

Gentle but consistent encouragement eventually led to her daughter using the room and after that Carroll says there was very real improvement.

Alex LeRiche's mural adorns the wall of the sensory friendly room. – © *Courtesy of J. René Roy*

"She realized she had the world by the tail. She had all the help she needed. Her marks were getting better and she just told them, 'Well, too bad you don't have this support,'" chuckles Carroll.

Carroll says everyone gets overwhelmed from time to time, and swinging in a hammock works a lot better than crying alone in a bathroom stall. Even Carroll will retreat to the rocking chair for a few minutes just to calm and refocus.

Years ago when she was feeling overwhelmed after dealing with the daily routine of an IR teacher, Carroll first identified the need for a sensory room. She just didn't have the time or drive to deal with what she thought would be a huge hassle.

In the end, she says it was much easier than she believed and would like to see such rooms in all schools, including post-secondary. She considers them just as necessary as a student library, gymnasium or washroom.

"I don't think it's something we should have to work so hard to go and get. I think it should have been provided to us," says Carroll. "It's not just autism, which is what some people don't get. All these kids in my room, they're not all autistic but they all use the room."

CHAPTER SEVEN
Inclusive community healthcare

Healthcare in more remote communities can differ substantially from larger urban populations. In Port-aux-Basques, the Dr. Charles L. LeGrow Health Centre, which operates as part of Western Health, is the hub of healthcare for the Southwest Coast.

More acute cases or those requiring more extensive treatment can be shuttled to larger hospitals in Corner Brook or even St. John's, but the regional hospital is the first stop when it comes to seeking medical treatment. Being familiar with the communities they serve, the medical professionals working at the local Health Centre are aware of the greater prevalence of autism in the immediate region.

It was perhaps inevitable that the hospital would seek out ways to help its patients beyond treating immediate medical concerns. Valerie Francis is a nurse working at Dr. Charles L. LeGrow Health Centre. Her 10-year-old son, Clifton, is autistic. Her experiences both personally and professionally have helped her recognize that more could be done to assist patients and their caregivers coming in for treatment.

"Obviously all my coworkers there know about Clifton," says Francis. "If I go in with Clifton they would ask me like 'What can I do to help' and they try to accommodate him the best they can while I'm there. But I'm thinking not everyone has this privilege."

Francis says it's not that her colleagues were unwilling to go the extra mile for patients, but that often they would be unaware that patients were autistic or dealing with anxiety or any other sensory issues.

"Going to the hospital is not something that is routine or planned or structured," notes Francis. She admits it was sometimes difficult to watch Clifton struggle when it came time for medical treatment. "It can be really overwhelming."

When Francis first moved back to Newfoundland from her home in Nova Scotia, staff were unaware. By telling them about Clifton's autism, it allowed her colleagues an opportunity to make small changes to accommodate him.

"Anyone with autism or anxiety, this is when they're vulnerable, you know?" says Francis.

One of her most recent experiences with taking Clifton in for medical care was a good experience, but Francis believes that was because staff already knew her son was autistic. Her colleagues allowed her to take Clifton to a unused treatment room to wait and Francis says it made a huge difference for him to have a calming, quiet space during the wait to see a doctor.

During another visit, a new doctor who was unaware that Clifton had autism tried to carry on as he did with other young patients by distracting him with small talk. Clifton is verbal and instead asked the doctor to explain procedures to him before carrying them out. Once Francis explained that her son needed to know the steps broken down the doctor was quick to comply, but it took Clifton actually asking first.

"If you go in, it never comes to you to say my son has autism or anxiety. You don't say that when you register. You're not asked that when you register, you know. So the need is not identified and staff is not aware," says Francis. "And what works for Clifton is probably not going to work for the next one either."

Since the town had been declared autism friendly and other businesses and facilities had adapted to become more inclusive, Francis wondered if the hospital might be able to follow suit.

Her first call was to Joan Chaisson to bring AIM on board and get some feedback on what steps, if any, could be taken to transform the Health Centre. Both Francis and AIM felt that a sensory room for patients to retreat to and some front line autism friendly training for the staff would prove beneficial. Francis also reached out the new hospital administrator, David Palmer, and the hospital's chief of staff, Dr. David Thomas.

"They were great. They were on board. They were really open to our ideas. They were just really ready and willing to co-operate," recalls Francis. "They thought it was a wonderful idea."

Francis says all of her colleagues at the hospital have been nothing but receptive, open and supportive. Palmer echoes that sentiment and adds that officials from Western Health were also quick to jump on board.

"It's certainly our goal to become more autism aware and autism friendly in the organization here as well, recognizing that our waiting area doesn't necessarily meet everyone's needs," says Palmer.

The hospital's first big hurdle was just finding space. The Dr. Charles L. LeGrow building is an older facility and has undergone somewhat extensive remodeling as its needs and services have grown. The administration realized that the space for a sensory room had to be relatively close to the registration and treatment areas, which restricted choices to the main floor.

Palmer had hoped to find room immediately adjacent to the main waiting area but that wasn't feasible. Instead he found a suitable space down a corridor near the building's entry way, next to some of the imaging rooms. This turned out to be advantageous as the corridor sees less foot traffic than the main waiting space.

"It was able to be tailored to different levels of sensory needs. So you wouldn't have the kind of sensory overflow from the waiting area into the room," notes Palmer. "I think it was a pretty easy choice for us to support the initiative once we found that there was space available."

Once they had settled on a suitable space, Palmer began looking for models in other healthcare facilities that he could draw on. He couldn't find any in Newfoundland and Labrador, and after more research found that there are actually only a few in the whole of North America, all of which were based on large hospitals in busy urban centres. There was really no existing model for a smaller healthcare facility serving a more rural population.

"We had a hard time finding spaces in health institutions to model ourselves on," admits Palmer.

Eventually Dr. Charles L. LeGrow staff, AIM and Western Health worked together in order to develop its own sensory room model. AIM had experience building sensory rooms in a school and a hotel, but building a sensory friendly room in a healthcare institution presented more unique challenges.

The room they had chosen was at a first glance entirely unsuitable. It had a tiled ceiling and standard commercial fluorescent lights. The walls were a dark brown, making the small room feel even tighter, and there were no audio capabilities or furniture. There was also a distracting patterned floor and a large, conspicuous wall heater that dominated the outer wall.

AIM advised the hospital that in order to become autism friendly, the room would have to be altered to have only clean lines, flat surfaces and softer lighting. That meant repainting the walls, changing the ceiling and flooring, installing new adjustable light fixtures, and building a custom bench seat for patients to sit on that would also serve to disguise the large wall heater.

"There's also a mural," says Palmer. "So that was a new thing to me. I wasn't aware of what would be seen as a sensory issue in terms of décor on the walls but actually it was the AIM group that had contacted the artist and provided some of the direction on the mural which is absolutely beautiful. As an individual I just find that scene to be very calming too. I'm hopeful that those who use that sensory space will also feel that way."

Not only did AIM purchase the paint for the room, the group also furnished it. That presented yet another set of challenges.

"Everything in the hospital has to be cleared by infection control. That was a big hurdle for us," admits Palmer.

To meet hospital cleanliness standards, furniture cannot be porous. That means no fabrics, cloths or soft materials. There could be no carpet or rugs on the floors. The furnishings also had to be easily movable and withstand high grade industrial cleansers.

As a result, AIM selected furniture from large suppliers like Home Hardware and IKEA made of plastic or imitation leather. The group also had to tweak its sensory kit. The new hospital kit had to not only fulfill sensory needs but also meet mandated cleanliness standards.

Just cleaning the room can present a challenge. Palmer says that in the future, he may have to explore what cleansers, if any, would still meet hospital sanitation standards, but perhaps offer a less overt reaction for those with chemical sensitivities who use the room. Then there is the hand sanitizer that is available to the public at key points throughout the hospital.

"It's a necessary evil to have these really strong cleaners here," he admits. "We will just have to see how that goes."

In addition to the cosmetic changes, the hospital also upgraded the audio equipment and installed a hard line telephone so that reception staff could call the room to advise waiting patients that the doctor was ready to see them.

Once the room itself was completed, the hospital and Western Health had to develop a procedure for assigning its usage. There is signage and other documentation posted at registration as well as the waiting room area stating that a sensory room is available in the hospital. Parents and caregivers must request access to the room, which is granted on a first come, first serve basis.

It remains, however, incumbent upon the patient, parent or caregiver to notify staff of any sensory-related treatment requirements. With AIM's help, Palmer has also tacked on additional training for staff who see patients at triage and treatment to ensure that they are using autism-friendly care practices. As the model is still being implemented, procedures are still being tweaked to determine what works best for patients and staff.

"We don't have standardized autism training for our organization which I think is another avenue for us," says Palmer. "I know that it's on our radar as an organization."

When it comes to the impact on the hospital's budget, Palmer says the bulk was mostly spent on labour. There were also material costs for the audio system and the custom bench that the hospital absorbed.

"Relative to health costs it wasn't that much," says Palmer, who considers the expenditure relatively minor when compared to the cost of an acute care patient on a ward. "It wasn't a tremendous cost relative to other health related costs. Realistically it would be the time and planning that would be the biggest hurdles and the space, I think, is the biggest hurdle as well."

One unforeseen consequence was that once the hospital had assigned a room for sensory usage there followed other requests for dedicated space for various needs. Naturally it is impossible to fulfill them all, particularly in a smaller facility. Palmer prioritized the sensory space and tried to accommodate other requests, such as employee wellness or professional training, in appropriate existing spaces that wouldn't require conversion. Palmer considers the sensory room advantageous for all of the hospital's patients.

"The advantage, as well, is that it's not only for clients who present with autism. It can be for anybody," he says. "You may think of a patient that has anxiety or, as an example, for anyone who is just unwell. Headache, migraine. You name it."

He also cites other models where sensory rooms have been used as a community outreach space and hopes to explore that in the near future also.

"I think that every institution would like to be more autism friendly and certainly have space to be tailored to other sensory needs if they could. I think in the business of healthcare sometimes you're doing so many other things that maybe it's just not on the radar or maybe there isn't the impact of the groups like we have with AIM here," says Palmer.

Palmer says that implementation in a healthcare setting is outright impossible without solid teamwork. Chaisson and AIM provided practical, experienced advice. Hospital staff overhauled the room, and medical personnel under Chief Dave Thomas developed and implemented new care procedures. When it came to the administration side of making the hospital sensory friendly, Palmer says Western Health personnel made it easy.

"They were all supporters of this as well. We really haven't had any organizational resistance. In fact, it's the opposite. Our organization would like to celebrate this as a model and see what else that can be done. It's interesting because we are doing a new facility in Corner Brook and it makes you wonder what can be incorporated into that."

The sensory friendly waiting room at the Dr. Charles L. LeGrow Health Centre in Port-aux-Basques is colourful and welcoming while still adhering to industrial and medical standards. Like the rest of the facility's common areas, this space is available to all clients not just those on the autism spectrum.

CHAPTER EIGHT
Focusing on the future

In order to get an official diagnosis of autism by a doctor, one of the specific criteria includes social communication difficulties.

Tony Leamon is a former educator who now works as a speech language pathologist. He provides assessment, therapy and consultation services for children and adults with any kind of communication issue, be it verbal or non-verbal. His goal is to help people understand and communicate with each other better.

Twenty years ago, around when Leamon first transitioned from teaching into speech language pathology, he might have seen one client on the autism spectrum. These days his caseload of clients with autism is much higher.

He says there's still lots of research underway to determine why there is such a significant increase. In reflecting on his own youth, Leamon recalls going to school with children who were labeled as intellectually disabled and he cannot say if they would be considered autistic by today's standards.

"Yes we've gotten better at diagnosing, but if we had the same diagnosing tools as now and I were to take them back to that day, I don't think the instance would have been as high as it is today," he says.

He concedes that he has no hard data to support this – just his own anecdotal experiences and observations. Four or five decades ago it was not uncommon for children with difficulties to be kept at home during the day, away from a formal education.

"Was it that some of these people never came to school?"

Leamon believes that with any real increase in awareness and exposure, as service and supports are put into place, it helps people with autism become a greater part of everyday society.

"As you open up these environments and they become comfortable in the environments, it makes sense that they're going to extend these skills into other environments. It does make a big difference for them," says Leamon.

He credits AIM with helping to open up possibilities for autistic children in the immediate region. He believes there will be a difference for children who can take advantage of these resources versus those in communities without such supports.

"That difference can be attributed to a few different reasons. One is the children themselves are being exposed to opportunities and experiences, and learning to use their skills in real-life environments," says Leamon. "In saying that, there still definitely needs to be transitional measures for these children as they become young adults and adults."

Leamon hopes that AIM will continue to implement resources to help today's children become part of the future workforce.

"As they become adults, what will they need?," asks Leamon, somewhat rhetorically.

Leamon goes on to explain that children will continue to require access to existing resources but that inevitable entry to the workforce will require additional supports.

"Will we facilitate that as well in our community?"

Leamon believes that the transition from high school into the workforce is currently the biggest challenge that people on the autism spectrum face, and notes that this has already also been recognized on a national and international scale.

He credits AIM for opening up its available resource areas to adults as well and has clients who have been invited to avail of them as needed. While AIM has achieved great things for early intervention and accessibility, Leamon maintains that government will have to play a greater role in the transition to adulthood.

For parents of children on the autism spectrum, or of any child with intellectual or developmental challenges, the worry about what happens to their child as they move into senior age is predominant. Leamon says there is no real support in place for the parents either.

"Of course it's impacted by financial ability," says Leamon. "People that are financially able, they start those transition plans early."

He recounts a story of parents who built an apartment on to their house for their intellectually disabled son and hired a support worker for him. They set boundaries, such as no popping next door unexpectedly, to further develop his daily routine and help him become more independent. But that kind of transition plan is simply not viable for parents without deep pockets.

"Those life skills are really important to the transition from that young school aged child to that older teenager – young adult."

Leamon says that's why early intervention and development, like taking an autistic child to the corner store to buy ice cream, is so critical. Exposing autistic children to only school-based type skills or exposing them to life skills at a later age may create gaps as they transition.

Autism is one area. I work with other children and that's one area of my caseload."

He points out that children with Down's Syndrome, for example, often face similar challenges. He would like to see more advocating for all of his clients who need these supports and resources, as opposed to just limiting it to people with autism.

For now AIM is facing those challenges as they develop. Building a sensory room at the local high school is just one example, and as the children move into adulthood Chaisson says AIM will continue to learn and grow with them to develop new support methods.

"To do that we're going to have to start working with the government," says Chaisson. "We're growing with the ones that we're representing in our group."

In the immediate region there are about 20 children AIM is trying to help, but via it's public Facebook page the group is also trying to help another 80 scattered across the country.

Looking ahead, Chaisson foresees more cooperative initiatives at the college level, and that will start first and foremost with educating herself on what is currently available.

In 2019, the provincial government released an Autism Action Plan. Part of that plan includes a pilot project similar to the School To Work Transition (STWT) that is designed to help those with intellectual disabilities, currently defined as having an IQ of 70 or below, find employment.

Section 2.9 focuses on community support services based on functional need rather than intellectual disability. To date this pilot project is underway in three different areas, with a goal of province-wide implementation by 2022.

Chaisson is also aware that some college programs allow students to work at their own pace, and for non-scholastic pursuits there are community employment programs available that can help adults on the spectrum support themselves financially. However, Chaisson notes that the existing programs can be difficult or confusing to access, and that will likely have to change if children with autism are ever going to become fully independent adults.

Chaisson says preparing for the future must begin in childhood and it must start with the parent. If the child has a public meltdown, for example, then it must become a learning experience instead of an excuse to retreat.

That is why AIM has developed so many resources for young children and is currently developing them for teenagers. Attempting to persuade an adult to engage with society after a lifetime of going to school and coming home and retreating to their room is extremely difficult.

"The parents have to get outside their box," insists Chaisson. "The kids have to get used to it too when they're younger."

Cathy Lomond wishes her sister Sherry, who has Down's Syndrome, had been able to harness some of these resources when she was a child. Instead Lomond's mother had to fight just to keep Sherry in school.

By age 50, when her parents died, Sherry was unable to live independently and required a new living arrangement. Since group homes had been abolished, she ended up living in a senior's complex. Lomond believes Sherry really didn't belong living with the elderly but at the time there was no alternative.

Even so, Sherry has found a way to survive and even thrive, becoming an unofficial caregiver for some of the residents by ensuring they get to the dining room to eat.

"My mother and my father devoted their entire lives to looking after Sherry," she says. "To a point that she probably should have been broken away from them years ago. She would have become, not a better person, but you know, the life skills where she could have been out on her own in an apartment. I know she's sharp enough for that."

Lomond says children today must be taught crucial life skills early on instead of relying on parents and caregivers who will eventually die.

Chaisson agrees. Ideally she would like to see a plan developed to assist with semi-independent housing once students have completed schooling and are moving into the workforce.

"They must be integrated into society," says Lomond. "It can be done."

CHAPTER NINE
Local government support

Back when AIM was first getting off the ground, the provincial Liberal party was still in opposition and the Conservatives controlled the House of Assembly. Once the Liberals gained power in 2015, Burgeo – LaPoile MHA Andrew Parsons, who represents much of the Southwest Coast region, was chosen as the new Justice Minister.

Back when he first started looking into autism, Parsons was still an opposition critic for health and education. One of the topics he was charged with researching was how the sitting government was dealing with autism.

"I would stand up in the House of Assembly and ask a question. And you start getting emails from people, and then you have people reaching out more and more," recalls Parsons.

As a consequence of the feedback and by continuing his research, his own awareness grew, and by the time AIM was up and running Parsons already had a pretty good grasp of what initiatives the province was actively funding. He was also aware that part of the Liberal's action plan for the future centered around autism.

When it came to local initiatives, it no doubt helped that Parsons and Joan Chaisson had been acquainted for many years prior to AIM's conception. He credits her as an invaluable resource in his education about autism, as well as the parents within the AIM group who willingly answered his never ending stream of questions.

"Part of my job is to help constituents," notes Parsons. "But I would have an interest in it, having done so much work and knowing the stats."

When Chaisson turned to him for financial help to fund purchases, Parsons understood the importance of the resources she was asking for and was able to help. He helped identify and procure provincial funding for sensory friendly gymnasium equipment for the Bruce II Sports Centre, for the elementary school playground, and for a variety of other AIM initiatives.

Parsons believes that AIM's work and his own efforts have also helped raise autism awareness within the provincial government parties itself.

"I don't know how many questions were asked in the House of Assembly prior to when I got there. I don't think it was as big a topic," says Parsons. "I like to think that every day that I stood up in the house and asked two, three, four questions, some people were watching. Some people were responding and it's just a general increase in that awareness. Some frustration too."

Parsons remembers feeling frustrated when challenging the sitting Conservatives about autism funding and being told that millions of dollars were already in place for initiatives.

"I was like – that's your problem. You're throwing money at it. You're not doing anything to figure out if it's actually working."

In fact, Parsons says many in the House of Assembly didn't fully understand why he was asking so many questions, but by then he had researched just how prevalent autism is in Newfoundland and Labrador and believed that things needed to change.

Using the House of Assembly as a platform to raise awareness or educate his peers didn't always endear Parsons to them either. Things got testy enough that at one point he was even heckled in session for continuing to advocate for further change.

"What if I was asking questions on cerebral palsy, if I was asking questions on alcohol addiction," shrugs Parsons, "That just shows the ignorance that existed. I think that's evolved. We're getting to a point now where there's nobody that's not aware."

Knowing what he does now about autism, Parsons says he sometimes reflects on his youth and wonders if some of his classmates were struggling with autism or other sensory challenges. Such reflection usually just prompts him to ask still more questions.

As his constituents reached out, Parsons not only learned about autism, he realized there was more that he could do in his role as MHA and more that government needed to do at the local level to help families and caregivers. His colleagues were also beginning to reach similar conclusions.

"A lot of times they try to pigeon hole issues. Same with Justice, saying this is a Justice issue. Well actually no. This issue actually belongs to Social Services, Health and Education. We just end up with it," he says. "Same thing. Then everyone would sort of peg it as a health issue, but no, this is an education issue. We need to provide supports to children and to teachers and educators. It just grew."

On a more personal level, trying to change things for his own constituents and also alter longstanding provincial policies on autism provided Parsons with greater job satisfaction. He felt more productive as things changed and he was able to do what he set out to do in the sometimes harsh political arena – help people.

"When people say why do you want to do that job? That's one of the reasons. There's that feeling that comes with it."

Helping people is a juggling act for many MHAs, particularly those with larger ridings. Parsons represents a large geographical riding that actually has a relatively small population.

He insists he does his best to help everyone within his demographic, and his sustained popularity inside and outside of his own riding certainly lends credence to that claim, but the fact remains that constituents must partner with government in becoming key advocates to effect lasting change.

"Sometimes the force and the persistence, as well as the ability of the person asking, dictates how successful it is, and that group is very good at it," notes Parsons. "And I say that because a lot of time people will come and ask for funding, for any number of things, and that's not just me. That's province wide."

Being able to explain in detail why the funding is so important and who it will serve only makes it that much easier for Parsons to petition for provincial monies. And if an initiative serves more people than just a single demographic, the application is more likely to be successful.

When the Bruce II and AIM partnered to bring in the sensory gym, it was to benefit all of the region's children and not just for children on the spectrum.

"You want to blanket as many people as you can with support," says Parsons.

Up until 2015 when he switched to the Justice portfolio, Parsons also dealt with the ASNL, which is an official registered charity and as such receives greater financial support from the provincial government.

He still advocates for more funding at cabinet or budget meetings, but as Minister of Justice his work with autism has switched to that of a more district level. Asking for money for sledges is a lot easier and more viable than asking for funding to construct a new building.

"You've got a million dollars worth of asks and you've got a hundred thousand dollars. How do you spend it?", he asks rhetorically. "It's persistence."

He also says there's a relationship that has developed and grown which underlies his work with AIM.

"It's not like they walked in one day and boom they're done, nor did they get something the first time they asked," says Parsons. "There's due diligence, now more so than ever. With the fiscal situation that our province is in you can't just hand out funding like you want to."

He has attended AIM meetings and other events to glean firsthand the work the group is doing and who it will benefit. Building the relationship has taken time and effort from both sides, but as a result Parsons believes it has made things easier for everyone to maintain that important due diligence when it comes to spending taxpayer money.

"To me it's not about giving money out. It's about investing money. What's the return on that going to be, and autism funding to me is something that has a return."

Parsons says investing in autism initiatives not only impacts the health and well being of those on the spectrum, but that of the families and caregivers as well. Children who are given more resources earlier on in life will eventually grow into adults, and Parsons is keen to help make them active, productive and successful adults.

How government can help do that on an overall provincial level is not something he will speculate on even as he recognizes it as a growing concern.

Instead he shares details about a chance conversation at a seminar in St. John's where he spoke to a senior with a son nearing middle age. The senior parent admitted to being scared for his son after he dies and will no longer be there to provide care.

Up until that moment, Parsons admits he was really only considering the needs of children with autism and not those of the adults on the spectrum, nor those of their caregivers.

Parents will eventually die or face their own health issues that will force them to step away from the caregiver role, and as more people are becoming properly diagnosed there will be an increased pressure on government, social services and the healthcare system to help families adjust.

"That's when it hits you," he admits. "There's a lot they can do but there's definitely supports that are needed."

Those supports will cost money and for a province currently grappling with the fiscal fallout of Muskrat Falls, energy rate mitigation and the COVID-19 pandemic, the financial outlook is bleak. Parsons says that just as people pick and choose what bills to pay or where to spend their money, government does the same on a larger scale and under far more scrutiny.

"Right now the output exceeds the input and there are more outputs coming," says Parsons.

He concedes that the province's demographics are playing a huge role in its financial future, which he labels as challenging at best if not scary at times. Newfoundland and Labrador has a rapidly growing senior population and the birth rate is on the lower end of the scale.

"It's realizing that there's not an endless pot of money," says Parsons.

One of the reasons he believes AIM is so effective is that their initiatives are not only helping children with autism, but they also aren't particularly costly. AIM's partnership with the business sector has strategically offset the need to delve into provincial coffers.

"That's teamwork."

CHAPTER TEN
Small scale fundraising

Like all of Canada's provinces, Newfoundland and Labrador has its own Autism Society to help citizens with autism. Officially registered government charities must distribute funds and resources throughout an entire province. Conversely, while Autism Involves Me does work to help children outside the immediate region, its primary focus remains on local residents with ASD.

The two organizations do work together regularly. ASNL has helped train AIM and local stakeholders and AIM donates funds from its annual Autism Walk to support ASNL.

Also of note is that ASNL has dedicated staff and employees to pay, while AIM has a board of three volunteer directors who receive no renumeration. That means that 100 per cent of the monies AIM raises goes towards procuring resources and developing other initiatives.

AIM is readily transparent on social media and via correspondence to donors about where every dollar goes.

After Joan Chaisson received a private donation from a supporter in Ontario, she purchased more sensory equipment with that money, then sent the anonymous donor a photo of the items so that the donor knew exactly how their money had been spent. She will also send donors a copy of the deposit receipt for funds into AIM's bank account.

"It lets people know that I'm not keeping this and putting this into my account," says Chaisson. "It's very much trust based."

When the group first began to actively fund raise, AIM also strategically partnered with other local groups to raise funds. For example, in partnership with the town's historical society, AIM was able to raise funds through a small lottery. The wind machine they will buy together, to be installed at the town's train museum, will benefit both groups.

Those with ASD will be able to feel the wind in a controlled environment, and tourists will be able to appreciate the strength of the infamous Wreckhouse. The Wreckhouse, situated not far outside of town and sandwiched between the Long Range Mountains and the Gulf of St. Lawrence, regularly experiences hurricane category winds that has toppled rail cars and transport trucks.

AIM continues to partner with the region's business community and schools, sometimes through one day special events or through ongoing, lengthy challenges.

In order to entice partnerships the end goal must be mutually beneficial. A business owner will want to make money, perhaps by increasing traffic through their store or increasing their overall exposure.

"You partner with somebody and that's the key to it really," offers Chaisson. "In order for this to work on our little budget or no budget that we have, number one is you have to go partners with somebody."

Once Hotel Port-aux-Basques became the first autism friendly hotel in Canada, it was featured in newspapers, and along with AIM received extra publicity by being featured in magazines and on national news platforms.

While it does fund raise independently, AIM prefers to work in partnership. This tends to increase exposure and bring in different segments of the population who may be more active within a different community group. People who don't attend the Annual Show and Shine fundraiser might instead choose to contribute when they visit the train museum.

AIM only actively campaigns when it is trying to meet a specific goal, usually to purchase a resource item they've identified as beneficial and worth the investment of time and money. One such example is fundraising to raise enough money to outfit seven fire department trucks with blankets and sensory kits. In a region with a population base of less than 10,000 residents, constant active fundraising is simply not feasible.

When there is no specific goal to be met, AIM's fundraising remains largely passive though no less important. Small displays at convenience stores, Hotel Port aux Basques, the local museum and an ongoing partnership with a local recycle depot where residents can take their recyclables and donate the return all certainly help.

If the bank account hits more than $1000 between active campaigns, AIM will use the funds to purchase something on a lesser wish list, such as another weighted blanket, or replace toys and equipment that have sustained some wear and tear.

One of the primary sources of funds for the group remains both public and private funding.

The province of Newfoundland and Labrador has a variety of grants available for sports, education and accessibility changes. The applications can involve a lot of paperwork but are worth the time and effort. GoodLife Kids Grants have also been an important resource in granting funds for the Little Fitness centre, the swimming pool and the sledges.

Research by AIM's directors, sometimes with key help from municipal and provincial representatives, has helped increase resources throughout the town, from inside the schools to the available equipment at the region's sports complex, which would otherwise be cost prohibitive to acquire.

SUGGESTIONS FOR ACTIVE, SHORT CAMPAIGNS

- Weekly toonie lottery (Split evenly between winner & AIM/Partner)

- Motorcycle Ride for Autism (donations solicited)

- Musical Concert for Autism (admission fees, 50/50 lottery)

- Show and Shine car wash (donations solicited)

- Yard sales (donated items by residents with proceeds to AIM)

SUGGESTIONS FOR PASSIVE, EXTENDED CAMPAIGNS

- Donation boxes at stores near registers

- Smaller crafted items for sale at partnering businesses

- Recycling centre refunds from donated cans and bottles

- Private, unsolicited donations (using social media triggers)

Some other ideas for fundraising may include book fairs, bake sales, sporting events and walks to raise awareness. Don't be afraid to brainstorm with people in your community or emulate other groups that have run successful campaigns.

Bear in mind that in order to fund raise successfully in a smaller community, it is best to give the public some down time between campaigns and to know the target demographic well enough to offer a wide variety of activities to appeal to different segments.

APPENDIX A
Sample: Guest Accommodation Checklist

Guests who wish to utilize a hotel's autism friendly resources should be offered the following questionnaire upon registration, ideally as an auto-responder form to complete via email. Supporting brochures and/or video links should also be offered at the same time.

In order to ensure that your stay in our autism friendly suites is more enjoyable, we ask that you please answer the following questions to allow us to better prepare for your needs.

1. Do you require any visual aids of the hotel prior to your arrival, such as photos or a video tour of the rooms?

2. Do you have any special dietary requests, allergies or food aversions?

3. Do you require a separate, quiet place for your meals instead of the hotel dining room?

4. Would you prefer a room with a kitchenette (hot plate, toaster, microwave) to prepare your own meals?

5. Is your family member prone to wandering? If yes, what advice can you offer on how staff best approach this person if they are observed without supervision?

6. Is your family member over/under sensitive to particular issues and if so what are they?

7. Will you require access to our sensory calming room, which is equipped to meet the needs of visitors with sensory challenges?

8. Are there any items in particular which you will require during your visit (a specific item to assist in the washroom)?

9. Are there any special circumstances or requirements not included above that our staff should be made aware of prior to your arrival?

APPENDIX B

Sample: Picture menu

KID'S MENU

	**Chicken nuggets and french fries**
	**Hamburger and french fries**
	**Pepperoni and cheese pizza**
	**Grilled cheese sandwich**

APPENDIX C
How to develop an autism resource binder

Before compiling a resource binder, it's important to note who it is intended for and how it will be used. For example, hotels may wish to include a binder for its guests in its autism friendly suites, while facilities and businesses might want to develop binders to keep near workstations or in staff only break rooms as training references.

It can also be helpful to keep copies of the facility's posted signage in the accompanying binder, and it is highly recommended to use colour pictures whenever possible, as visual aids tend to be much more memorable than long lists of data.

Here are some suggestions on types of resources you may wish to include:

• a list of your on-site resources, including designated and trained staff, posted sensory hours and safety information

• a list of any nearby businesses and facilities which are sensory friendly, including maps to their locations, their daily schedules, and their contact information and links to their websites

• a copy of the sticker displayed by local businesses and facilities as autism friendly for easy identification

• location of sensory kits in local facilities and the hours which they can be accessed

• an overview of autism and sensory processing disorders, including an explanation of how the senses are affected, to help increase awareness

• a list of sensory challenges, how to recognize them and how staff can quickly help, as well as a list of what not to do in commonplace situations

• a copy of the business training materials, including the quick reference handouts included in Appendix E: Autism Awareness for Business. *(see page 109)*

• relevant information about autism such as misconceptions, statistical data and links to helpful websites

Many websites will offer downloadable information you can include, but when developing a resource binder, be careful not to infringe upon any copyrights.

APPENDIX D
Overview: becoming autism friendly

In order for a business or facility to become autism friendly, a series of steps must be completed. The following examples are currently used by AIM and are designed to help with implementation, but as businesses are unique these serve as a readily adaptable guide.

1. Business owners, managers and employees are invited to sign up for a free autism awareness training session. Initial session is usually large, but a large scale business with a significant number of employees may wish to have an on-site private training session. Front line staff who do not attend must be trained by the employee(s) or employer who completed training. Upon successful completion business is awarded an 'We are Autism Aware' sticker.

2. Staff are to complete an on site evaluation of the business and implement changes using the reference materials and checklists received during the first level training session. Employees should work together to brainstorm any additional initiatives not covered during the meeting, and changes should be documented on provided checklists for review by AIM.

3. After preliminary review of submitted checklists, schedule meeting with AIM re: implemented changes, discuss any further necessary changes or suggestions, and what resources AIM can offer or would like to see brought into the business. If the business is part of a franchise or chain, this will likely necessitate hard copy letters of approval from head office.

4. Decide on a firm, specific date for completed implementation and on-site AIM review. During regularly scheduled employee meetings (i.e. weekly), ascertain that appropriate progress has been made and staff are fully trained. Make sure all employee questions and concerns are addressed prior to visit.

5. During the on-site visit, AIM personnel will interact with staff so they can check service and amenities to determine if clients will indeed feel comfortable and staff will be able to meet their needs, especially should a meltdown occur. After a successful visit, the business will receive an official 'We are Autism Friendly' sticker and larger wall sign to certify the business is considered officially autism friendly.

APPENDIX E
Autism awareness training for business

A first level autism awareness presentation for business opens with a short presentation on autism and communication. Whenever possible, after this introduction, invite a guest speaker to share a relevant personal experience story.

Sharing allows business owners to better understand the experience of daily living with autism and how even minor efforts on their part can impact current and future customers.

The overall presentation itself is kept short but highly informative, highlighting the most important points for attendees without overwhelming them.

Trainees are given copies of the material to help design and implement their own strategies and to keep in their businesses for future reference.

Presenters may also choose to use a slideshow to accompany the written materials that includes relevant regional statistical data and images.

Upon successful completion of the first level of business training, attendees will receive a 'We are Autism Aware' sticker which they may display at their business or facility.

The information included in this sample is currently used by AIM in the first stage of its business training, but the basic structure can be used as a template for customization.

PRESENTER'S INTRO

Consider this a short crash course in Autism 101, where we will be discussing some things which you can do to help facilitate interactions with customers who may have autism. We will highlight the main points but will not go into detail in order to save time to answer questions and explore what steps you can implement in your place of business.

WHAT IS AUTISM?

Autism is a developmental disorder which affects language and communication, sensory processing and motor skills, and social interactions.

When a person is diagnosed with autism, it does not mean that they are developmentally delayed. There are some who may also be diagnosed with an intellectual delay, but bear in mind these are two completely different diagnoses.

For example: not all blind people are intellectually delayed. As with people who are blind, there are people who are diagnosed with autism who have extremely high I.Q.s.

Scientists know that the autistic brain develops differently from birth. This means that autism is just another way of seeing the world. They know there is a genetic connection, but they also believe there is very likely some type of outside environmental factor that is part of the cause. This factor currently remains unknown.

Autism has no cure. It is a lifetime disorder. However with early intervention, education, presentations, work friendly environments, autism friendly towns and communities, more autistic children can grow up to be independent professionals in society.

It has been stated that autism is referred to as a disability because our society is not designed to work with people who have autistic brains.

LANGUAGE AND COMMUNICATION

Fifteen to twenty per cent of people who have autism do not develop oral speech. Thus they require an alternative communication system such as PECS (Picture Exchange Communication System), typing on an iPad, sign language, etc. Again, many people believe that because a child is non- verbal then they are intellectually delayed. This is not true.

(Introduce guest speaker to share a relevant story.)

It is important to remember that these children can hear you, understand what you are saying and remember how you reacted to them and treated them. Some people will eventually develop speech only to lose it when they develop anxiety, as anxiety and autism go hand in hand. These are the people who you may encounter in your business and they require one-on-one interaction.

Eye contact can trigger their anxiety. For some, talking is one of the hardest things for them to do, so their speech is sometimes the first thing to shut down.

Some children have echolalia where they repeat things others have said or what they have heard on TV. These phrases would not fit in the communication at the moment they are saying it, but the phrases are usually meaningful to the speaker.

For example, if a child says, "The sun is shining" and their mother or caregiver affirms this by saying, "Yes, the sun is shining", this may actually indicate a desire to go outside.

Then there are people on the autism spectrum with fluent speech.

Many people with autism have a difficult time understanding what is being said to or asked of them. Again, this is not because of an intellectual disability.

It takes some autistic people 30 seconds or longer to process what was said to them. If you grow impatient and repeat your question or statement, they must begin processing your words all over again from the beginning.

For example, if you were to say, "That costs $5.95 please," it may take them some time to react. If you repeat it, that will delay their comprehension and the transaction even longer. Any rephrasing or attempts to hurry the transaction on your part before they have processed the request will likely trigger their anxiety, which in some cases can shut down their speech completely.

Alternatively, the customer may respond with, "You get it" and you may believe they have an intellectual delay while in fact they are trying to extricate themselves from your place of business before they succumb to a meltdown due to the stress and anxiety.

When in such a situation, it would be more beneficial to show the customer the price on the cash register or write it down for them on a piece of paper. Remember, visual communication always works better than oral when serving people with autism.

One common characteristic of people with autism is hyper focus, which is an intense focus on one subject. For example, one young gentleman visits a lot of stores and he has a very strong interest in hockey memorabilia. Take a few moments to talk to the gentleman about this subject.

He is not interested in how your displays look, what you have in stock or what is on sale. However, he still needs to interact with you and he will always appreciate the person who chats with him about his interest or merely listens and agrees with what he is saying.

SENSORY PROCESSING AND MOTOR SKILLS

Many people who have autism are also diagnosed with a sensory processing disorder. They process information and use their senses differently. They may be more sensitive or less sensitive to everyday sounds, smells, lights and textures and may require more time to adjust to an environment.

A grocery store is one of the most difficult places for people on the autism spectrum to visit. There are a great many different smells and textures, changes in lighting, loud speaker announcements, numerous conversations at different volumes, cash registers and other ambient sounds that they must process.

For example, in AIM's hometown of Channel-Port aux Basques there are two grocery stores. Some parents of children with autism prefer taking their child to Store A instead of Store B.

When entering Store B, the cash registers are very close to the main entrance. Noise from the registers, the clattering of the carts and people chatting can be an immediate sensory overload for the child.

In contrast, at Store A, the main entrance opens into the produce section, away from the registers, so the child has time to slowly adjust to the new environment before moving towards the queue at the registers.

There are two other sensory factors that are not commonly discussed but are crucial for people with autism: proprioceptive and vestibular. In essence, the proprioceptive sense allows your body to know where you are in a space and how much pressure you are applying to something. The vestibular sense is your sense of balance and stability.

We will continue to use a grocery store in our example, this time for a child who is under sensitive.

If you see a customer pushing the shopping cart harder than usual and even bumping into things, they may be having difficulty with their proprioceptive sense. Being under sensitive, they may not realize how hard they are pushing the cart and need to push it quite hard in order to feel pressure going from their hands to the cart's push bar. They may also not realize how close they are to obstacles or other people, and will have to bump hard to process the fact that they have hit someone or something with the cart.

You may also spot someone engaging in a repetitive motion, such as rocking back and forth on their feet, flapping their hands, tapping their fingers, twirling, shaking a string or something in front of their face, and so on. These people are stimming.

These actions are self-calming and very important to someone with autism. It helps them regulate their senses, process their environment and helps them think clearly. One way to help someone is to keep fidget items handy in a sensory bin that customers can access should they feel the need.

When someone has too many sensory triggers at one time, they will have a meltdown. This is where their brain shuts down, and this can happen to both children and adults.

Meltdowns usually begin with anxiety.

The person may start stimming to try to process what is happening and if this doesn't work they will want to leave the environment. You may notice that the person may become very quiet or alternatively they may get loud and scream.

Parents and caregivers usually know what behaviours to look for but there are times when it becomes impossible for them to help the person with autism leave your place of business before the meltdown stage.

Please check with the parent or caregiver to see if you can provide any assistance. Do not engage with the person in the meltdown, as they have lost all cognition. They will have to go through the meltdown just as someone with epilepsy would have to endure a seizure. Do not stare or make unkind remarks about parenting or misbehaving. After the meltdown is over, please be aware that the person is very likely to be feeling quite tired, embarrassed and thirsty.

A meltdown is NOT a temper tantrum. Do you know the difference between the two? *(see page 109)*

A tantrum occurs when a child cries or shouts excessively, but is still quite aware of where they are, what they are doing and why they are doing it. They have control over their actions. They will usually check to see if they are being watched. If they are successful in getting what they wanted during the outburst, the behaviour is immediately stopped.

In contrast, someone with autism who is experiencing a meltdown cannot think clearly for themselves and sometimes cannot see or hear, which can leave them feeling terrified. Their brain is overloaded with sensory triggers and has shut down in much the same way as your computer will crash when you push the same key over and over or give it too much information in a short time span.

Many with autism have difficulty reading another person's body language, which is a common way we communicate, whether it's by moving our hands, eyes or even our entire bodies. People with autism do not like to use eye contact and do not pick up on social cues.

They may begin to process what you are saying but then may get a whiff of a smell that they either hate or love and thus causing them to forget what you are saying. They can also confuse their emotions, laughing inappropriately at a tragic story or negative experience you have shared.

For someone with autism, they have to first process what you've said, match it with a past experience they recognize as being similar to what you've relayed, and then figure out how to respond to you all in a matter of seconds. Sometimes they get the wrong emotion.

People with autism do not like sudden changes.

For example, if they have their mind made up that they want a cookie and there are none left, their whole world may turn upside down. Neurotypical people have coping skills in these situations but since someone with autism does not, it is very hard for them to generalize their skills.

Instead, they require coping skills for different experiences and that is truly difficult, if not outright impossible. They do learn which coping strategies work best for them but this takes time and a great deal of hard work.

Again, please remember that visual aids are quite beneficial. Write down what they need to know in very short, clear notes with main details – especially if something has changed since the last time they did business with you.

In closing, I wish to share: when you have met one person with autism, you have met just one person with autism. No two people with autism are alike but you can still do things to help everyone feel comfortable in your place of business.

Please take these worksheets and sample materials home and read through it bearing in mind the knowledge you have received here.

If your organization would like to proceed to the Autism Friendly certification, we can arrange a one-on-one meeting at your location to ascertain what specific changes we can implement there, as well as any further necessary employee training.

TANTRUM VS. MELTDOWN
How to recognize the difference

TANTRUM

Goal Oriented

The individual has a specific goal that they want by exhibiting this behaviour.

Watchful

Individual watches reaction of caregiver to determine likelihood of success and may change intensity or nature of behaviour accordingly.

Injury Avoidance

Individual can cognitively think of ways not to hurt themselves during behaviour.

Ends Quickly

If goal is achieved or individual tires the behaviour stops.

Self-control

The individual is aware of and in charge of their behaviour the entire time.

Warning Signs

Desires a particular outcome and when faced with inability to achieve it, escalates behaviour.

MELTDOWN

No Goals

No demands are made before or during the behaviour.

Not Watchful

The individual has no interest in how others react.

Possibility of Injury

Individual cannot cognitively process likelihood of injury and is only reacting.

Slow to End

Lasts longer, slowing down only as individual becomes comfortable.

No Control

Individual is experiencing sensory overload, resulting in survival mode thinking style and thus not aware of or in control of their behaviour.

Warning Signs

Differs in individuals. May become quiet, may begin stimming, may cover ears or eyes, may try to run away or escape environment.

PRO-ACTIVE AUTISM CHECKLIST

Indicate if idea will be implemented & when completed

Y / N	SUGGESTION	DONE
	Dim lights.	
	Turn music down or off. Eliminate or reduce background and repetitive noises (i.e. fans, air conditioners).	
	Prohibit perfumes and scents (i.e. cleansers).	
	Keep a pair of noise-reduction headphones readily available for complimentary use for customers with sensitivities.	
	Pre-determine hours when noisy equipment will be prohibited (i.e. vacuum cleaners, loud music, movement of larger items).	
	Schedule a sensory friendly time (usually one hour per week).	
	Post info about sensory times in high visibility areas, website and social media accounts.	
	Post photos and videos on your website so caregivers and customers can become familiar with your business prior to visiting.	
	Send photos of yourself or staff directly to caregivers and customers if advised of an expected visit beforehand (i.e. accommodation).	
	Explain routines in short, clear steps (i.e. haircuts, medical exams).	
	Stock a sensory kit for customers to use during their visit.	
	Use paper towels in the bathroom. If possible, remove dryers. If not, post signage asking patrons not to use them during sensory hours.	
	Advise on website, social media and high visibility signage of any expected or planned changes to routine, event and/or business.	
	For events, post exactly what is being planned and abide by it.	
	For events, use a different colour wristband or stamp to alert staff of guests who may require extra help.	
	For events, explain to event workers and guests beforehand what autism is and what to expect. Be sure to include children.	
	Have guests on the spectrum arrive early to slowly acclimatize to the noise and group rather than after festivities have begun.	
	Remind sensory guests they can leave early. Keep their departure bag and belongings nearby and easily accessible to facilitate exit.	

Y / N	SUGGESTION	DONE
	Avoid bright and/or unusually patterned staff uniforms.	
	For schools and churches, post internal, external and social media times for scheduled bell ringing.	
	Public facilities (i.e. libraries, pools) should have rules and guidelines clearly posted.	
	Children's menu items should use photos including the dinnerware that will be used. Give short, accurate descriptions of the food.	
	Display upcoming menu changes well in advance and not on the day of implementation (social media, restaurant chalkboard, etc.)	
	Post immediately and clearly when a daily special becomes unavailable or is sold out.	
	Have a table, booth or area in the establishment with less décor (sensory stimuli).	
	Fence in playgrounds and other play areas.	
	For accommodations: pre-determine any specialty food brand or other items that can be stocked in advance.	
	During renos or construction consider accessibility. Larger toilet stall, changing table, adult bench, hoist system, non-slip floor, etc.	
	Borrow or purchase educational resources for staff and customers. Keep them easily accessible for quick reference.	
	Employ staff who are on the autism spectrum.	
	Teach all staff autism awareness and service methods.	
	Solicit suggestions from public and staff via a suggestion box.	
	Persist. Continue to invite and accommodate guests with special needs even if the initial turnout is low.	
	Avoid construction, shelf restocking and cleaning during sensory hours. Post signage when scheduling during non-sensory hours.	

RE-ACTIVE AUTISM CHECKLIST
Use the following tips to better assist customers.

TRAINER INITIALS	TIPS FOR SUCCESSFUL INTERACTIONS	EMPLOYEE INITIALS
	Do not insist upon eye contact.	
	Do not stare. Do not make assumptions.	
	Respect how individuals choose to refer to their autism.	
	Understand stimming behaviours and do not overreact to them.	
	Understand that because a behaviour is bad does not make a child or person bad. Do not judge the parent/caregiver or customer.	
	Know the difference between a temper tantrum and a meltdown. Do not interfere but when possible quietly offer help.	
	Do not warn something will happen unless it is a known certainty as opposed to just a (strong) likelihood. Avoid possibilities.	
	Understand that new environments take a huge amount of effort for people on the autism spectrum. Be patient.	
	Understand that tasks neurotypical people find straightforward can take a huge amount of effort for people with autism.	
	Do not touch people without warning or permission. Instead use praise or offer a small treat as a reward.	
	Keep talking to a minimum so as not to overwhelm. Listen to the customer and let them take the lead. Keep listening.	
	Do not insist upon an action (i.e. removing an item of clothing) if it makes them uncomfortable or anxious (within reason).	
	Do not repeat questions. Do not rephrase questions. Allow extra time for customer to process the information. Be patient.	
	Do not use metaphors, similes, idioms and sarcasm.	
	Do not guess the answer. Do not attempt to coax or pry a response or choice. Be patient.	
	Use literal language and provide a clear choice. Avoid open ended questions. Be patient.	
	Use tools whenever possible (iPads, paper, picture menus), especially for non-verbal customers. Visual supports can be highly effective.	
	Enter their world by engaging them about a special interest or activity they are currently undertaking.	
	Understand negative, aggressive reactions are signs of anxiety. Ask caregivers what may be triggering it and correct them if possible.	

TRAINER INITIALS	TIPS FOR SUCCESSFUL INTERACTIONS	EMPLOYEE INITIALS

What are some things you can do as a business owner to change or add within your environment to help someone with autism?

1. _____

2. _____

3. _____

4. _____

5. _____

6. _____

7. _____

8. _____

9. _____

10. _____

APPENDIX F
Sample: stickers and signage

Signage can be customized, but if it is recommended to keep the group or service branding consistent to help clients and caregivers readily identify participating facilities and businesses. Use bright, eye catching colours and easy to read typeface.

First level stickers, like this one, are usually quite inexpensive to produce on a home office printer using sticky back sheets readily available at office supply vendors. Alternatively, you may wish to partner with a local printing company to defer costs, especially for the second level mounted signs, which usually also list the daily sensory schedule.

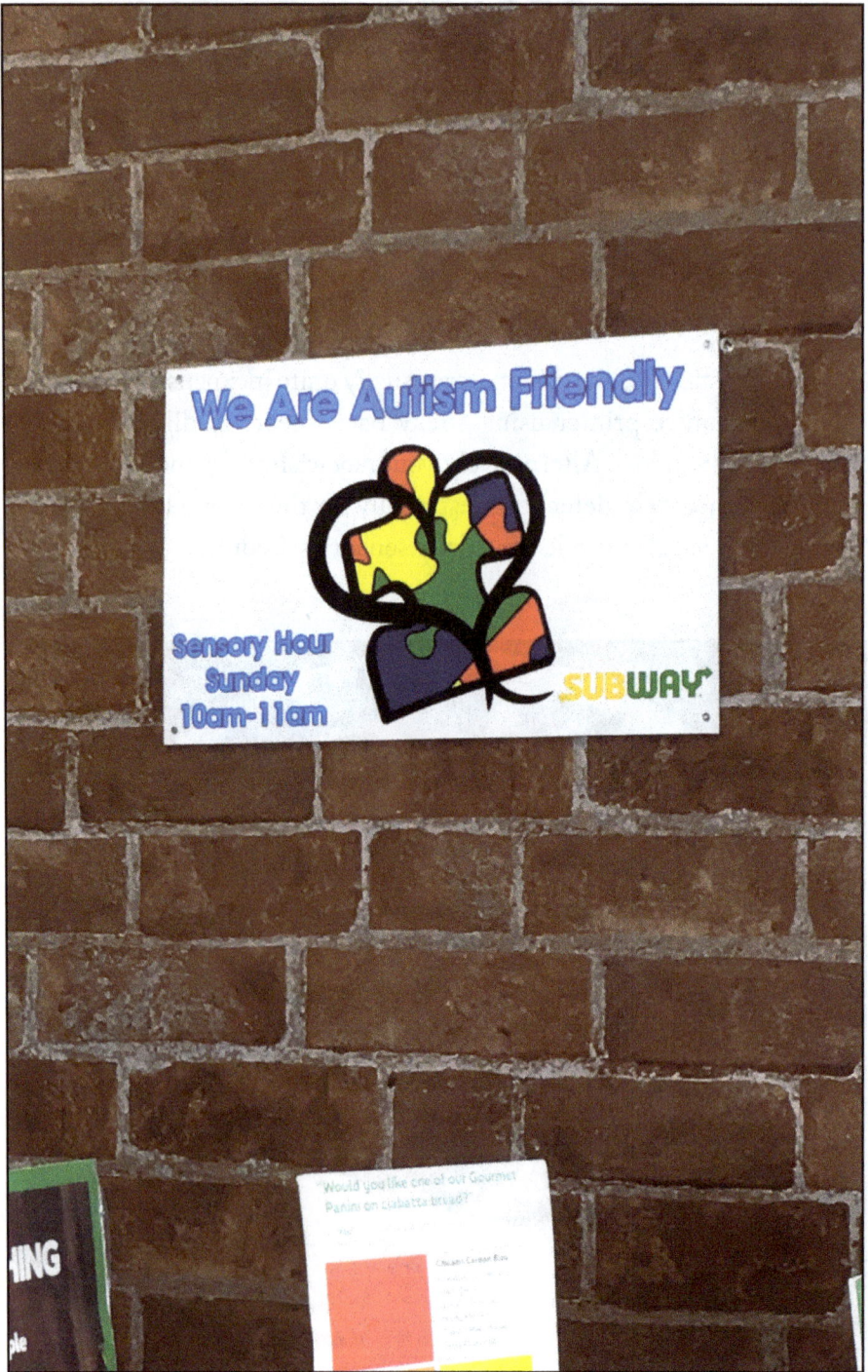

© Courtesy of J. René Roy

APPENDIX G
How to build a sensory kit

All sensory kits are not the same, nor are they all suitable for every business or facility. For example, hospital kits must comply with detailed sanitation regulations, which means no porous items can be included.

Sometimes blankets, visual aids (i.e. colour changing plastic lights) and musical objects will be added depending where the kit will be placed and what is best suited to a particular environment.

The goal of every kit is to offer items to meet a variety of sensory challenges, particularly visual, auditory, and tactile needs. Dollar stores usually have many small, affordable items suitable for making kits.

Once completed, it is advised to attach an information card with contact details to the lid of the kit. Kits should be checked regularly so that lost and damaged items can be replaced.

The following examples are meant only as guidelines.

INFORMATION CARD

One in sixty eight children are diagnosed with having autism. Since the brain is wired differently, we must remember: if a child with autism cannot learn the way we teach, then we must teach them in a way they can learn. Sensory overload is very overwhelming for these children. It would be like us trying to watch all 500 channels on TV at once, with the volume turned on blast.

Suggested Items:

Spring coil, sunglasses, flashlight, crayons, miniature pinball game, fidget spinner, toy truck with spinning wheels, hand wipes.

Suggested Items:

Noise reduction headphones, ear buds, slow rising squishy ball (white),

red rubber band, Tigger head, squeezable firm ball (blue),

hard rubber skeleton, soft rubber dragon puppet.

Suggested Items:

Notepaper, pencils, PlayDoh, textured pipe cleaner, stretchable items including a heart shaped slinky, hourglass timer, yellow tube with movable ball insert.

Completed Kit:

All of the items identified in the previous three photos are included in the final kit. Contact & info cards are attached to the lid of the kit.

APPENDIX H
How to build a sensory room

Although any size room can be developed into a sensory room, proper planning is one of the most important steps. Here are some things you need to know before getting started.

Who will be using this room?

Think about the people who will benefit. Determine their ages, needs and physical challenges. Young children will need different equipment and supplies than teenagers or adults. Does your intended group have any physical challenges that will have to be addressed?

Draw up a list of potential business partners.

Engaging the business community helps offset the cost of resources while increasing their own client base and profile, usually by offering a suitable room or through the donation of money and resources, and can even help with fundraising initiatives.

Assess the intended location.

Is it readily accessible at any hour or only at certain times? Is the room in a high traffic area or a low traffic one? How nearby are staff? Is there an intercom system or telephone in the room? Is there wifi available for a smartboard? When the room is locked, who will hold the access key or swipe card? What physical changes, such as new painting or lighting, will have to be made? Does the building have regulations it must abide by that will have to be taken into consideration?

Determine your budget.

New equipment and supplies can be cost prohibitive. How will you pay for these items? What fundraising initiatives can you use? Are there government or private grants available to help offset costs?

Based on the criteria you've identified, draw up a practical solution strategy. Include details such as the room schedule, especially if it is located in a facility that will likely have other clients using this room, like a sensory gym accessible to the public.

Develop a wish list of changes, equipment and supplies with no financial or regulatory limits in mind. The room should offer items to meet needs in the following categories: visual, auditory, olfactory, gustatory, oral, tactile, proprioceptive, and vestibular.

Visual:

• Dimming lights

• Fiber optic or LED lights. Bear in mind that for some people, flashing lights may trigger a seizure.

• Sunglasses

• Mirror

• Light table activities

• Glow in the dark stars and planets

• Bubbles

• Spinning toys

• Tornado tubes

Auditory:

• Musical instruments

• Buzzers (each with a different sound)

• White noise machine

• Quiet water fountain

• Noisy toys (with different sounds)

• Low noise fan

• Audiobooks

Olfactory (smell):

• Scented PlayDoh

• Scented markers

• Essential oil scents for alertness – lemon, peppermint, pine

• Essential oil scents for calmness – lavender and chamomile

• Scented bubble gum

• Scratch and sniff stickers

Gustatory (taste):

• Spicy and salty treats

• Different flavours of candy – fizzy, tangy, sour or sweet

• Crunchy treats such as carrots

• Soft treats such as marshmallows

• Sectioned plates to divide foods of different textures

• Picture menus on the wall

• Crafting edibles that the client can create then eat

Oral:

• Bubble blowing

• Milkshakes with a straw

• Vibrating or hard toothbrushes

• Sippy cups

• Harmonicas

• Unflavoured chewing gum

Tactile:

• Containers with different types of materials – rice, beans, feathers, cotton balls, marshmallows, sand, water

• Shaving cream (for painting)

• Kinetic or magnetic sand

• Edible PlayDoh

• Textured cards

• Blankets made of different materials

• Feathered archways

• Play tunnel constructed of different materials

Proprioceptive (relating to stimuli that are produced and perceived, especially those connected with position and movement):

- Trampoline

- Pea pod (allows client to feel pressure)

- Weighted vests

- Weighted blankets

- Hammock

- Crow's nest swing chair

- Therabands

- Heavy items to push or pull

- Cushions

Vestibular (balance and stability):

- Rocking chair

- Swing

- Climbing wall

- Spinning desk chair

- Balance beam

- Slide

- Yoga ball

- Balance bike or plasma car

- Teeter totter

Some of the suggested items may serve more than one need, and are also suitable for sensory kits. Choose items that can be easily cleaned or sanitized.

Furniture items that can double in use – such as a table with a storage compartment – are preferred. Chairs can be a place to sit but also meet a sensory need, like a beanbag chair or a rocking chair.

APPENDIX I
Recommended suppliers

Local businesses are highly recommended as the first stop when it comes to purchases. Dollar shops usually have a wide variety of items that can help with building a sensory kit, while hardware stores have door chains and drawer locks for accommodation upgrades. Larger retailers like IKEA and Home Hardware may also have furniture suitable for sensory rooms, like bean bags or colourful plastic tables and chairs.

For other equipment and materials, you may wish to consider some of the following suppliers:

TFH Canada
Sensory and special needs toys.
specialneedstoys.com

Flaghouse
Sport, recreation and special needs.
flaghouse.ca

Wintergreen Learning Materials
Free resources and virtual catalogs.
wintergreen.ca

Yogibo
Family fun furniture and accessories.
yogibo.com

Kan-Go-Roo Playgrounds
Sensory friendly playground equipment.
kangoroo.com

Windco Flags
Flags, windsocks and banners.
windcoflags.com

Privacy Pop
Pop up bed tents for nap time, bed time, playtime and alone time.
privacypop.com

FatBoy Canada
Furniture, lighting and accessories.
fatboycanada.com

VoxxLife
Specialty athletic and lifestyle wear, including socks and insoles.
voxxlife.com

Scholars Choice
Educational resource materials for teachers, parents and daycares.
scholarschoice.ca

Scholastic
Book publisher & distributor focused on children and education.
scholastic.ca

Proloquo2Go
Augmentative and alternative communication resources.
assistiveware.com

Teachers Pay Teachers
Teaching resources and lesson plans for educators.
teacherspayteachers.com

APPENDIX J
Recommended reading

INFORMATIONAL BOOKS

I Am in Here – The Journey of a Child with Autism Who Cannot
Speak but Finds Her Voice
by Elizabeth M. Bonker & Virginia G. Bremen

The Way I See It by Temple Grandin, Ph.D.

Understanding Autism for a Dummies by Stephen M. Shore, Ed.D.
& Linda G. Rastelli, MA

The Official Autism 101 Manual - created & compiled
by Karen L. Simmons

Calm the @@@@ Down! A Day in the Life of an Autism Mom
by Florence Strang

The Reason I Jump by Naoki Higashida

The Asperger's Answer Book by Susan Ashley, PH.D.

Adult Asperger's Syndrome b Kenneth Roberson, PH.D.

Adolescents on the Autism Spectrum by Chantal Sicile-Kira

Playing, Laughing and Learning with Children on the Autism
Spectrum by Julia Moor

Understanding Autism through Rapid Prompting Method
by Soma Mukhopadhyay

The PRT Pocket Guide Pivotal Response Treatment for Autism
Spectrum Disorders by Robert L. Koegel & Lynn Kern Koegel

Pivotal Response Treatments for Autism – Communication, Social &
Academic Development by Robert L. Koegel & Lynn Kern Koegel

101 Great Ideas for Teaching & Raising Children with Autism or
Asperger's by Ellen Notbohm & Veronica Zysk

No More Meltdowns by Jed Baker, Ph.D.

From Anxiety to Meltdown by Deborah Lipsky

How Do I Teach This Kid To Read by Kimberly A. Henry, M.S.

Ten Things Your Student with Autism Wishes You Knew
by Ellen Notbohm

Challenging the Myths of Autism by Jonathan Anderson, Ed. M.

Autism The Gift that Needs to be Opened
by Autism Society, Newfoundland and Labrador

The Sensory Processing Disorder Answer Book
by Tara Delaney, MS, OTR/L

Raising Kids on the Spectrum – Chicken Soup for the Soul
by Dr. Rebecca Luanda

Raising a Sensory Smart Child
by Lindsey Biel, M.A. OTR/L & Nancy Penske

The Out-of-Sync Child, Recognizing & Coping with
Sensory Processing Disorder by Carol Stock Kranowitz, M.A.

The Out-of-Sync Child Has Fun. Activities for Kids with
Sensory Processing Disorder by Carol Stock Kranowitz, M.A.

Sensational Kids. Hope & Help for Children with
Sensory Processing Disorder by Lucy Jane Miller, Ph.D., OTR

House Rules (Fiction) by Jodi Picoult

Living with Autism day-by-day. Daily Reflections & Strategies to
Give You Hope and Courage by Pamela Bryson-Weaver

More Than Words- Helping Parents Promote Communication &
Social Skills in Children with Autism Spectrum Disorder
by Fern Sussman

Talk Ability – People Skills for Verbal Children on the Autism
Spectrum – a Guide for Parents by Fern Sussman

It Takes Two to Talk – a Practical Guide for Parents of Children with
Language Delays by Jan Pepper & Elaine Weitzman

Helping Your Child with Autism Spectrum Disorder – A Step By
Step Workbook for Families
by Stephanie B. Lockshin, PH.D., BCBA, Jennifer M. Gillis. MA.
BCBA & Raymond G. Romanczyk, PH.D., BCBA

Speak, Move, Play & Learn with Children on the Autism Spectrum by Lois Jean Brady, America X Gonzalez, Maciej Zawadzki & Corinna Presley

Autism Preparation Kit for Teachers by Bec Oakley

A Practical Guide to Autism – What Every Parent, Family Member and Teacher Needs to Know by Fred R. Volkmar & Lisa A. Wiesner.

The Organized Child – An Effective Program to Maximize Your Kid's Potential In School and In Life by Richard Gallagher, PhD, Elena G. Spira, PhD & Jennifer L. Rosen last, PhD.

How people with Autism Grieve, and How to Help by Deborah Lipsky

Autism Equality in the Workplace by Janine Booth

Stress Free Kids by Lori Lite

Could it be Autism by Nancy D. Wiseman
The Upside of Stress by Kelly McGonigal, Ph.D

Awesomism! A New Way to Understand the Diagnosis of Autism by Suzy Miller

The Oasis Guide to Asperger Syndrome by Patricia Romanowski Basha & Barbara L. Kirby

Autism a Practical Guide to Improving Your Child's Quality of Life by Jonathan Tommey and Polly Tommey

Understanding Death and Illness and What They Teach About Life –
an interactive Guide for Individuals with Autism or Asperger's and
Their Loved Ones by Catherine Faherty

Unlocked – A Family Emerging from the Shadows of Autism
by Susan Levin

The Weighted Blanket Guide by Eileen Parker and Cara Kosinski

The Loving Push – How Parents and Professionals can Help Spectrum
Kids become Successful Adults
by Temple Grandin, Ph.D. & Debra Moore, Ph.D

An Adult With an Autism Diagnosis – A Guide for the Newly
Diagnosed by Gillan Drew

Asperger's and Adulthood – A Guide to Working, Loving and Living
with Asperger's Syndrome by Blythe Grossberg, PSY.D.

A Full Life with Autism by Chantal Sicile-Kira & Jeremy Sicile-Kira

The Basic Reading Comprehension Kit for Hyperlexia and Autism
by Pam Britton Reese & Nina C. Challenner

Supporting Pupils on the Autism Spectrum in Primary Schools –
a Practical Guide for Teaching Assistants by Cary Canavan

Hands-On Activities for Exceptional Students – Educational &
Pre- Vocational Activities for Students with Cognitive Delays
by Beverly Thorne

Behavioural Interventions for Young Children with Autism – a
Manual for Parents & Professionals, edited by Catherine Maurice

A Work in Progress – Behavior Management Strategies and a
Curriculum for Intense Behavioural Treatment of Autism
by Ron Leaf & John McEachin

Life Skills Activities for Secondary Students with Special Needs
by Darlene Mannix

FOR CHILDREN / ADOLESCENTS

Potty Paloma – a step by step guide to using a potty by Rachel Gordon

Functional Sequencing Activity Sheets for Daily Living Skills
By Candy Schraufnagel & Amy Crimin, M.S. Ed., MS. Psy

I Have Autism, Autism Don't Have Me! By Tiffany Carter

My Friend with Autism by Beverly Bishop

Social Rules for Kids by Susan Diamond, PhD, BCET

Uniquely Wired by Julia Cook

Everybody is Different by Fiona Bleach

Oh Brother! Growing up with a Special Needs Sibling by Natalie Hale

I Have Needs Too! By Elizabeth A. Batson

Some Kids Have Autism by Martha E. H. Rustad

Autism Is....? By Ymkje Wideman-van der Laan

I See Things Differently by Pat Thomas

My Autism Book by Gloria Dura-Vila & Tamar Levi

The Autism Acceptance Book by Ellen Sabin

The Autistic Puppy by Darlene White Antle

Ethan's Story: My Life with Autism by Ethan Rice

A Friend Like Simon by Kate Gaynor

We're Amazing 1, 2, 3! A Story About Friendship & Autism on Sesame Street by Leslie Kimmelman

Ian's Walk – A Story About Autism by Laurie Lears

Can I Tell you about ADHD? By Susan Yarney

Can I Tell you about Asperger Syndrome? By Jude Welton

ASD and Me by Teresa DeMars

101 Life Skills Games for Children by Bernie Badegruber

101 Games & Activities for Children with Autism, Asperger's and Sensory Disorders by Tara DeLaney, M.S., OTR

Attention Games 101 Fun, East Games that Help Kids Learn to Focus by Barbara Sher

Early Intervention Games by Barbara Sher

Autism & PDF Adolescent Social Skills Lessons
by Pam Britton Reese & Nina C. Challenger

The New Social Story Book 15th Anniversary Edition with sections
for pre-school children and young adults by Carol Gray

Autism – What Does It Mean to Me. A Workbook about Self
Awareness and Life Lessons for Kids with Autism or Asperger's
by Catherine Faherty

Autism & Reading Comprehension Ready to use Lessons for Teachers
by Joseph Porter, M.Ed.

Visual Recipes – A Cookbook for Non-Readers by Tabitha Orth

Visual Supports for People with Autism by Marlene J. Cohen, Ed.D,
BCBA & Donna L. Sloan, M.A., BCBA

The Autism Friendly Guide to Periods by Robyn Steward

The Autism Playbook for Teens
by Irene McHenry, PhD & Carol Moog PhD

The Asperger Teen's Toolkit by Francis Musgrave

A Volcano in my Tummy – Helping Children to Handle Anger
by Elaine Whitehouse & Warwick Pudney

Andy and his Yellow Frisbee by Mary Thompson

The Girl Who Thought in Pictures: the Story of Dr. Temple Grandin
by Julia Finley Mosca

Hello, My Name is Max and I Have Autism by Max Miller

My Name is Emily I am Ten and I Have Asperger's Syndrome. An
Autobiography typed by my Mom.
by Mary Restivo & Emily Margaret

Different Like Me. My book of Autism Heroes by Jennifer Elder

Temple Did It, and I Can, Too! By Jennifer Gilpin Yacia
All Cats Have Asperger's Syndrome by Kathy Hoopmann

Welcome to my World – I Have Autism by Kay Fotsman

Please Explain Anxiety to Me
by Laurie Zelinger, Ph.D. & Jordan Zelinger, MSED

The Mindful Turtle – Teaching Coping Skills to Kids
by Florence Strang, B.A., B.Ed, M.Ed

My Family's Changing – a first look at family break up by Pat Thomas

When Mom and Dad Divorce by Emily Menendez-Aponte

It's Not Your Fault, Koko Bear by Vicki Lansky

I Miss You – A first look at Death by Pat Thomas

When Dinosaurs Die – A Guide to Understanding Death
by Laurie Krasnoyarsk Brown & Marc Brown

Who Has What? All about Girl's Bodies and Boy's Bodies
by Robbie H. Harris

Asking About Sex & Growing Up – A Question-and-Answer Book
for Kids by Joanna Cole

Amazing You – Getting Smart About Your Private Parts
by Dr. Gail Saltz

Tom Needs To Go – a book about how to use public toilets safely for
boys and young men with autism and related conditions
by Kate E. Reynolds

The Boy's Guide to Growing Up by Terri Couwenhoven, M.S.

What's Happening to My Body? A Book for Girls by Lynda Madaras

What's Happening to My Body? A Book for Boys by Lynda Madaras
It's Perfectly Normal – Changing Bodies, Growing Up, Sex and Sexual
Health by Robbie H. Harris & Michael Emberley

An Exceptional Children's Guide to TOUCH Teaching Social and
Physical Boundaries to Kids by Hunter Manasco

The Survival Guide for Kids with Physical Disabilities & Challenges
by Wendy L. Moss Ph.D & Susan A. Taddonio D.P.T.

WORKBOOKS FOR ADOLESCENTS

What to do When Your Brain Gets Stuck by Dawn Huebner, Ph.D.

What to do When Your Temper Flares by Dawn Humber Ph.D.

What to do When You Worry Too Much by Dawn Humber Ph.D.

The Anxiety Workbook for Kids
by Robin Alter, Ph.D., C Psych & Crystal Clarke MSW, RSW

Social Success Workbook for Teens
by Barbara Cooper MPS & Nancy Widdows MS

Executive Functioning Workbook for Teens
by Sharon A. Hansen, MSE , NBCT

Anxiety Workbook for Teens by Lisa M. Schab, LCSW

Don't Let Your Emotions Run Your Life for Teens
by Sheri Van Dijk, MSW

The Shyness and Social Anxiety Workbook for Teens
by Jennifer Shannon, LMFT

Body Image Workbook for Teens by Julia V. Taylor, MA

Self- Esteem Workbook for Teens by Lisa M. Schab, LCSW

APPENDIX K
Video resources

For more information on Channel-Port aux Basques and to view its autism-friendly resources in action, visit these clips on Youtube.

Today's Parent Magazine:
Canada's Most Autism-Friendly Town – World Autism
Awareness Day 2018

CBC News: The National
Meet the most autism-friendly town in Canada

Your Morning
This Newfoundland town is the most autism-friendly town in Canada

Ted Talks: Adam Harris
What is an autism-friendly community?

GLOSSARY

ABA - Applied Behaviour Analysis

AIM - Autism Involves Me

ASC - Autistic Spectrum Condition

ASD - Autism Spectrum Disorder

ASNL - Autism Society of Newfoundland and Labrador

BRUCE II - A regional sports complex serving the entire Southwest Coast of Newfoundland. The facility features a swimming pool, running track, bowling alley, curling rink, skating rink, weight room and executive meeting rooms.

CEC - Community Employment Corporation

GROS MORNE - a national park of Canada designated as a UNESCO world heritage site

IR - Instructional Resource

MARINE ATLANTIC - The Crown corporation passenger ferry service running between Channel-Port aux Basques and North Sydney, Nova Scotia. In the summertime the ferry service also offers a route from Nova Scotia to Argentia, Newfoundland.

MHA - officials representing an electoral district within the province of Newfoundland and Labrador are considered a Member of the House of Assembly, which is located in the provincial capital city of St. John's

MUSKRAT FALLS - a hydro electric dam project located on the Churchill River in Labrador. Significant cost overruns are projected to push taxpayer increases beyond affordable rates, which in turn prompted the sitting provincial government to open a public inquiry. The final six-volume report: "Muskrat Falls: A Misguided Project" is available online.

NLAF - Newfoundland and Labrador Association of Firefighters

PAB - Port-aux-Basques. Though the town is officially called Channel-Port aux Basques it is often only referred to as Port aux Basques.

RNL - Recreation Newfoundland and Labrador

SENSORY (disorders, sensitivities, overload, triggers) - the brains of people with sensory processing issues have trouble filtering, organizing and interpreting information and may experience extreme reactions to sights, sounds, smells, tastes and textures.

STIMMING - self-stimulating behaviour (usually a repetitive behaviour or spoken word or phrase) employed to help oneself soothe or calm

STWT - Provincial pilot program called School to Work Transition. It assists people with intellectual disabilities, which is currently defined as having an IQ of 70 or below. Employers hire students and are accompanied by an Employment Support Worker and any additional supports, or alternatively employers may choose to receive a subsidy, which can cover up to 100 percent of the wages.

TOONIE - nickname for Canada's two dollar coin

ABOUT THE AUTHOR

R. L. Roy is a former community journalist, sports reporter and graphic artist whose work has appeared in Atlantic Canadian newspapers and hockey magazines. Her story on Canada's first autism friendly hotel went viral, drawing national and international attention to AIM's work to increase autism awareness and inclusion.

After spending over two decades in Halifax, Nova Scotia, Roy returned to her hometown in Newfoundland. When she's not writing, she enjoys watching her beloved Montreal Canadiens, hiking the coastline or sitting around the fire with friends and sipping a glass of merlot.

Roy is a multi-genre author who also writes fiction and memoir. Her historical western romance novel, Ride a Wild Horse, is available via Amazon and her website at Wreckhouse Press. Her humour memoir, 6 Ways From Sunday, highlighting her frequent, disastrous road trips around Atlantic Canada is slated for release in Fall 2020. This is her first non-fiction book.

Twitter: @tygerlylly • *Facebook:* WreckhousePress
e-Mail: info@wreckhousepress.com

Thank you for reading!
Please consider leaving a review on Amazon, Bookbub or Goodreads.

Sharing your thoughts, whether positive or negative, is vital for independent authors, and is always greatly appreciated.